501 Enchanting Embroidery Designs

Irresistible Stitchables to Brighten Up Your Life

BOUTIQUE-SHA

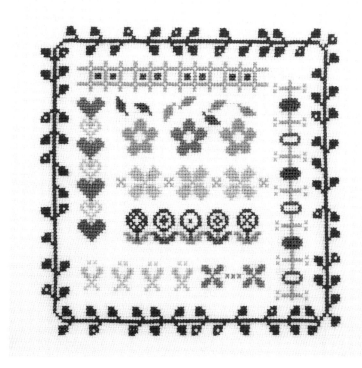

TUTTLE Publishing

Tokyo | Rutland, Vermont | Singapore

CONTENTS

PLEASE NOTE:

The designs in this book were embroidered on Lecien brand linen or cross-stitch fabric, using Cosmo brand embroidery floss, but you can substitute your own favorite fabrics and floss brands. Be sure to adjust your strand count to suit the thickness and texture of your fabric if necessary.

See the inside back cover for a chart converting Cosmo brand floss colors to DMC, a popular brand found in most U.S. craft and fabric shops.

A Scandinavian Cityscape

Design and embroidery by Sanja Harumi

Instructions given on **page 49**

Cute Cups

Design by Ozaki Tamami
Embroidery by Yoshizawa Mizue

Instructions
given on
page 50

A Cosy Room

Design by Nunomushi
Embroidery by Nakata Reiko

Instructions given on **page 52**

A Tidy Kitchen

Design and embroidery by Minato Kaori

Instructions given on **page 54**

A Visit to the Flea Market

Design by Nunomushi
Embroidery by Yoshizawa Mizue

Instructions given on **page 56**

Scandinavian Forest Designs

Design by Nunomushi
Embroidery by Nakata Reiko

Instructions
given on
page 58

Little Scandinavian Sketches

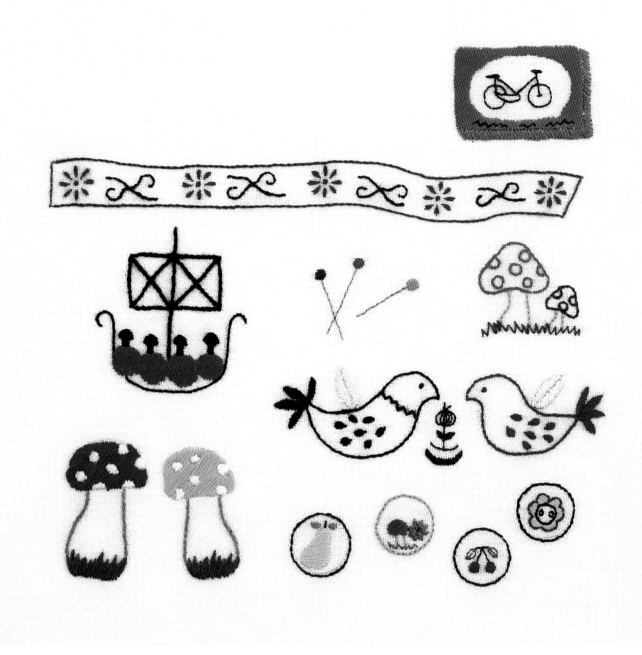

Adorable Items from Eastern Europe

Design by Koma Keiko
Embroidery by Yoshizawa Mizue

14

Instructions
given on
page 60

Sweet Little Sketches

The Music's Playing

Design and embroidery ✳ monkton*chiccoro

Instructions given on **page 62**

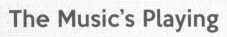

I Love Fruit!

Design and embroidery ✳ monkton*chiccoro

Instructions given on **page 64**

18

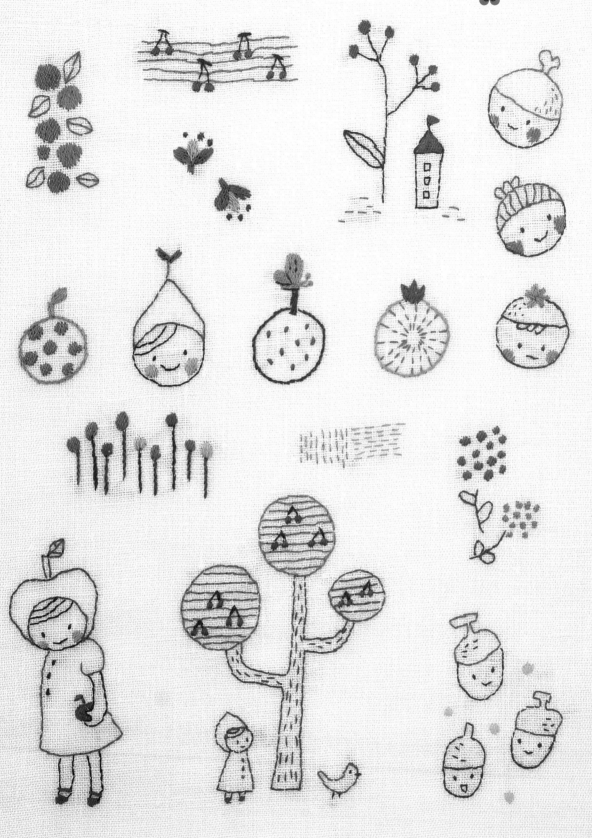

Sweet Things for Girls

Design and embroidery by sentiment doux

Instructions given on **page 66**

Stripes and Polka Dots

Design by Ozaki Tamami   Embroidery by Kanamaru Kaori

Instructions given on **page 68**

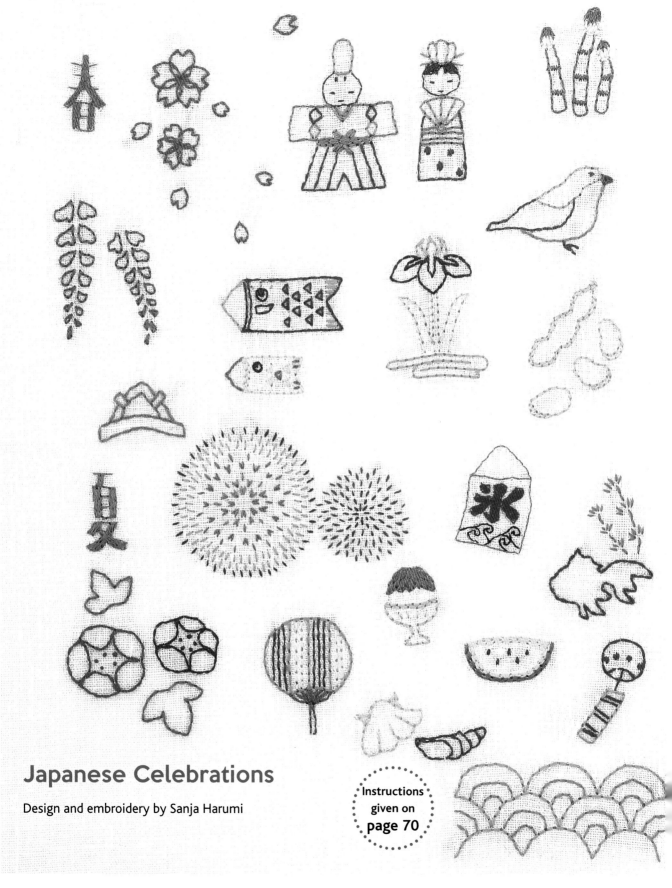

Japanese Celebrations

Design and embroidery by Sanja Harumi

Instructions given on **page 70**

秋

冬

Birds & Flowers

Design by Nunomushi   Embroidery by Yoshizawa Mizue

Instructions given on **page 72**

Tasty Tea Time

Design by Nunomushi   Embroidery by Yoshizawa Mizue

TEA TIME!!

Instructions given on **page 74**

Lace Patterns

Design and embroidery by Minato Kaori

Instructions given on **page 76**

✳ Cross Stitch Motifs

Scandinavian Style Cross Stitch

Design and embroidery ✳ Stitch Garden by Narukawa Kazuyo-Sumiyo

Instructions given on **page 78**

A Cross Stitch Alphabet

Design and embroidery by soeur*2

Instructions
given on
page 80

Cross Stitch Dogs and Cats

Design and embroidery by necca

Dog-1

Instructions given on **page 82**

Dog-2

Cat-1

Dog-3

Cat-2

Cat-3

Dog-4

Cat-4

Cat-5

Dog-5

Dog-6

Cat-6

Continuous Cross Stitch Patterns

Design and embroidery ✳ Stitch Garden by Narukawa Kazuyo-Sumiyo

Instructions given on **page 84**

Let's Embroider

Add a touch of embroidery to favorite little items and some sweet stitches to handmade accessories. Little motifs in your favorite colors create original pieces.

Instructions given on **page 86**

Pouches in various sizes are handy for everyday use and great for travel. Have fun choosing the little embroidery motif to show the intended contents of the pouch.

Stylish Pouches

Embroidery design by sentiment doux   Creation by Etsu Tanaka

Sewing Items

Embroidery design by 4—7 Keiko Koma
8—10 Stitch Garden by Narukawa Kazuyo-Sumiyo

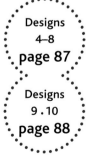

Designs
4–8
page 87

Designs
9 . 10
page 88

Cross stitch on linen creates these chic pin cushions and scissors case. Motifs in cute, pretty colors are recommended for the little self-cover buttons.

4   5

6   7

Button covers

8

Scissors case

9

10

Pin cushion

12

11

Add your own signature embroidery to simple store-bought camisoles. The little continuous patterns look lovely in one color, while the solitary flower motif is sweet in a pretty shade.

Instructions
given on
page 88

Signature Stitching on Camisoles

Embroidery and design by sentiment doux   Creation by Ono Michiko

Travel Companions

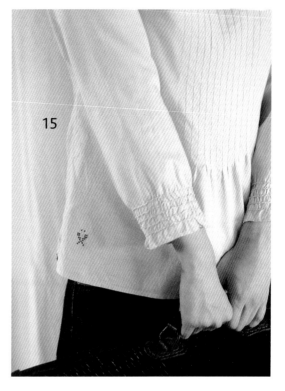

15

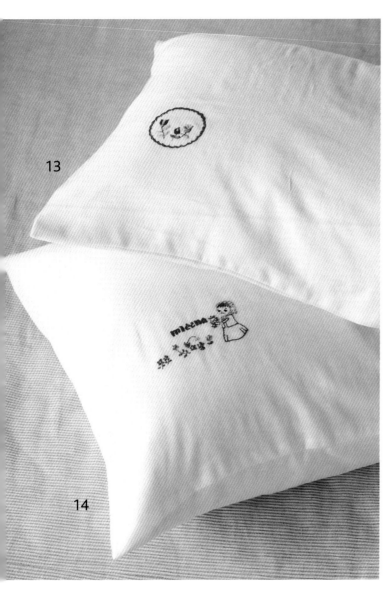

13

14

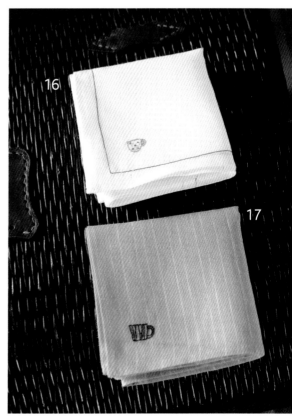

16

17

Embroidery design ✳ 13 • 14 by Keiko Koma   15 Stitch Garden by Narukawa Kazuyo-Sumiyo
16 • 17 by Nunomushi   Creation by Nishimura Akiko

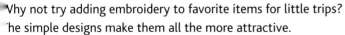
Why not try adding embroidery to favorite items for little trips?
The simple designs make them all the more attractive.

Pillow cases

Designs
13 .14
page 89

Blouse

Designs
15
page 90

Handkerchief

Designs
16 .17
page 90

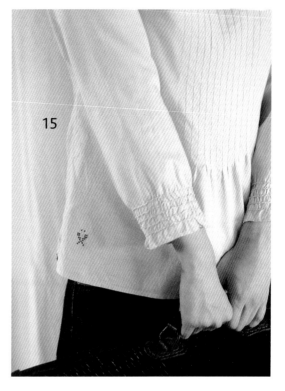

18

This cute set features a pyramid-shaped tea cozy with an apple motif, while the teapot mat sports an apple core embroidered in cross stitch. The running stitch down one side of the tea cozy makes it easy to fold.

Instructions
given on
page 92

19

Running stitch down the side lined in check fabric makes the tea cozy easy to fold

Apple Motif Tea Cozy and Teapot Mat

Embroidery design ✳ Stitch Garden by Narukawa Kazuyo-Sumiyo
Creation by Sakata Miyuki

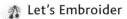

Dishcloth and Apron

Embroidery design by Nunomushi

A favorite solitary motif stars on a dishcloth, while lovable animals decorate a café apron with tape strings attached. In this way, a store-bought dishcloth becomes a unique item of your very own.

21

20

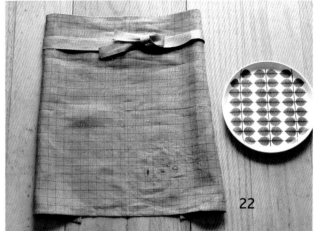

22

Instructions given on **page 91**

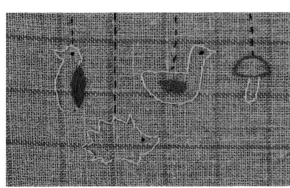

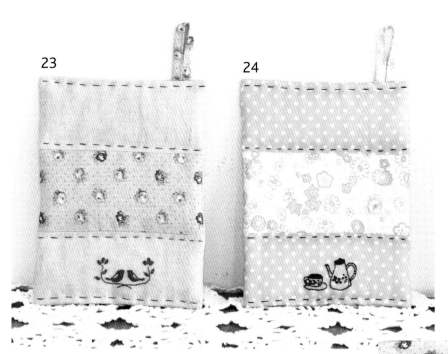

23 24

Pot Holders for a Budding Chef

Embroidery design by sentiment doux
Creation by Sakata Miyuki

Bird motifs and a tea set are embroidered
on soft shades for these pot holders. The
decorative running stitch along the seam
lines serves to make items easier to grasp.

Instructions
given on
page 93

Napkins for Adults and Kids

Embroidery design by Keiko Koma
Creation by Chiba Mieko

25 26

Instructions
given on
page 94

These napkins are ideal for wrapping around a lunchbox or to take
out on a day's hiking. The adult's
napkin features a thermos flask
motif, while the kids' version sport
cutlery and a cup.

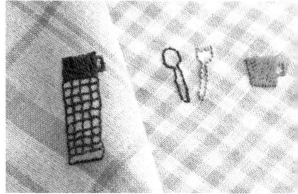

Butterfly Shaped Pot Holders

Embroidery design by Ozaki Tamami
Creation by Nishimura Akiko

Instructions given on **page 95**

he rounded lines of these pot holders make them look like utterflies. They feature embroidery of a cup and saucer or a poon, with a ribbon added as an accent.

Embroidery of a rounded basket motif features on this cloth which can be used to lightly cover items in a basket. The blue line is an effective accent.

Holders Basket Cloth

Embroidery design by Keiko Koma
Creation by Chiba Mieko

Instructions given on **page 94**

Embroidery Techniques

These are the basic techniques and equipment required for embroidery.

Equipment

↑ No. 25 embroidery thread (Cosmo embroidery thread) ★
This six-strand embroidery thread has its color number displayed on the paper band.

←Embroidery hoop ★
An embroidery hoop keeps fabric taut for neat results.

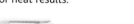

↑ Dressmakers pencil ★
Use for drawing designs directly onto fabric. Marks disappear in water.

←Carbon paper ★
Use to transfer designs to fabric. Marks disappear in water.

↓ Thread scissors ★

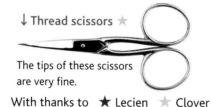

The tips of these scissors are very fine.

With thanks to ★ Lecien ☆ Clover

↓ Embroidery needles ☆
Embroidery needles have large eyes for easy threading.

Cross stitch needle linen fabric | French embroidery needle

The tip of a cross stitch needle is rounded (left)

Fabric

Linen Fabric

It's possible to embroider fabrics of all kinds including cotton and linen, but close-weave fabrics that are not too lightweight are most suitable. Open-weave fabrics can cause embroidery to warp, and if fabric is too lightweight and transparent, knots made on the wrong side of the work can be seen from the front.

Transferring Designs

■ Transfer using a dressmakers pencil

If you can see the design through the fabric laid over the top, you can trace directly over it onto the fabric.

■ Transfer using carbon paper

With paper carbon-side down on fabric and the design placed over the top, trace the design with a ballpoint pen. It may be a good idea to place cellophane over the design so the paper doesn't rip.

The transferred design. Fine details can be filled in later by referring to the original design.

Using No. 25 Embroidery Thread

1

Find the end of the thread from the skein of embroidery thread.

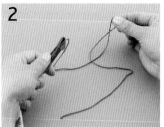

2

Pull out the thread, keeping the paper band lightly in place with one hand. Cut thread at about 15¾ in (40cm).

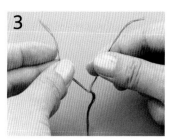

3

Separate threads. Unravel threads one at a time before placing desired number together for use.

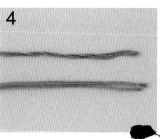

4

The threads at the bottom have been unraveled and placed together, while the threads at the top have not been unraveled. Threads that have been unraveled and placed together again allow for a neater end result.

Threading the Needle

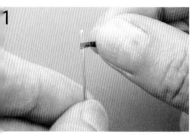

1

Wind the thread around the eye end of the needle and create a sharp fold.

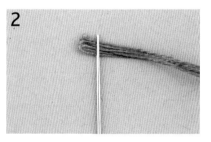

2

Pass the folded section of the thread through the eye of the needle.

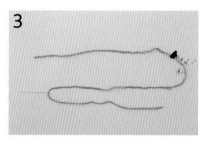

3

The threaded needle.

Starting to Embroider

1

(WS)

Confirm the placement of the design and position fabric firmly within the embroidery hoop.

2

(RS)

The fabric stretched within the embroidery hoop. Make sure fabric is taut.

3

(RS)

Pass needle from wrong side to right side of fabric.

4 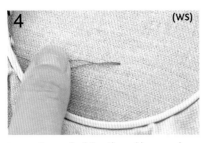 (WS)

Leave the end of the thread long and hold in place on the wrong side of the fabric.

5  (RS)

Pass needle through to right side of fabric and draw firmly before passing through to wrong side of fabric. This completes the first stitch.

6  (RS)

Continue sewing, making sure all stitches are the same length.

Finishing Off

1 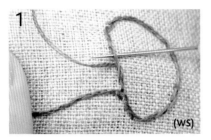 (WS)

Pass needle through to wrong side of fabric, working under and over completed stitches so the end of the thread is secured.

2  (WS)

Cut thread. Pass end of thread that was left long at the start through the needle and secure in the same way before trimming off.

Removing the Design

 (RS)

Once embroidery is completed, press a damp cloth or paper towel over the design to remove any marks, then leave to dry naturally. Be aware that ironing the design may reactivate the ink and cause it to become indelible.

Embroidering a Line

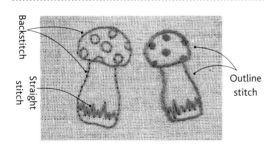

Backstitch and outline stitch are commonly used stitches. Outline stitch is created by working a line of diagonal stitches, so it makes a thicker line than backstitch.

Embroidery to Conceal a Surface

Satin stitch

This stitch plays up the luster of embroidery thread. Make sure thread is not twisted when creating this stitch.

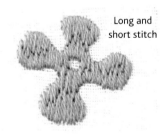

Long and short stitch

This is a series of stitches that join together, making it ideal for covering large areas.

How to Embroider

Outline stitch
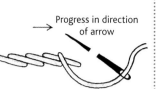
Progress in direction of arrow

Running stitch
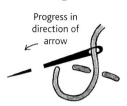
Progress in direction of arrow

Backstitch
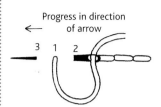
Progress in direction of arrow

3   1   2

French knot stitch

Wind 1–3 times around needle

Blanket stitch
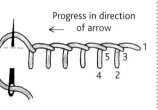
Progress in direction of arrow

1
5   3
4   2

Chain stitch
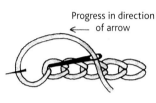
Progress in direction of arrow

Straight stitch

1   2
3
5   4

Cross stitch
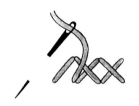

Long and short stitch
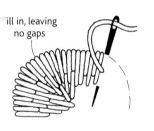
Fill in, leaving no gaps

Satin stitch
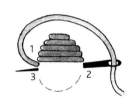
1
3   2

Seed stitch

Make stitches at random

Lazy daisy stitch
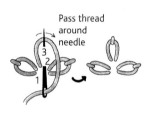
Pass thread around needle

3
2
1

Bullion stitch
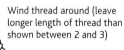
Wind thread around (leave longer length of thread than shown between 2 and 3)

Pull thread

1 Out
3 Out
Out   2 In

2
4 In

Cable chain stitch
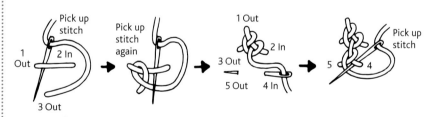
Pick up stitch
1 Out   2 In
3 Out

Pick up stitch again

1 Out
2 In
3 Out
5 Out   4 In

Pick up stitch
5   4

Chevron stitch
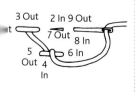
3 Out   2 In   9 Out
7 Out   8 In
5 Out   6 In
4 In

Repeat 2–9 times

Couching stitch
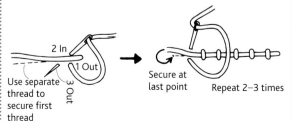
2 In
1 Out
3 Out
Use separate thread to secure first thread

Secure at last point

Repeat 2–3 times

Herringbone stitch
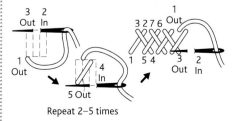
3   2
Out   In
1 Out
4
5 Out

1
Out
3 2 7 6
1   5 4   3   2
Out   In

Repeat 2–5 times

47

Cross Stitch

■ Starting to embroider

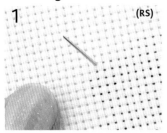

1 (RS)

Pass needle from wrong side to right side of fabric.

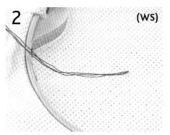

2 (WS)

Leave the end of the thread at least twice the length of the needle.

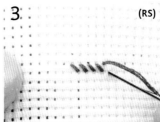

3 (RS)

Holding the end of the thread in place with your finger, make several stitches in a downwards direction only.

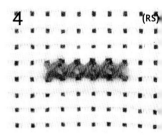

4 (RS)

Return to the start of the row by working stitches in an upwards direction, thereby completing the cross stitches.

■ Finishing off

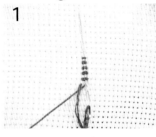

1

Pass needle through to wrong side of fabric and through the row of stitches.

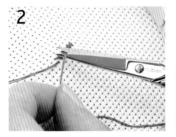

2

Cut off thread.

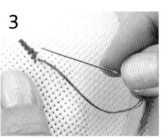

3

Thread remaining length of thread through needle and secure in the same way before trimming off.

■ Keeping stitches even

Make all your crossover stitches from the same direction.

When Using Fabric Other Than That Meant for Cross Stitch

Waste canvas

A grid-like mesh type of material called waste canvas enables cross stitch to be carried out on fabric which has a weave that makes it hard to count threads.

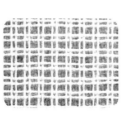

With thanks to Lecien.

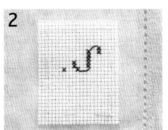

1

Cut a piece of waste canvas to a size larger than the embroidery design and baste it to the fabric.

2

Embroider over the waste canvas.

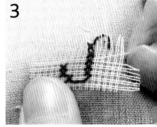

3

Remove basting and trim remaining waste canvas before removing weft threads one at a time.

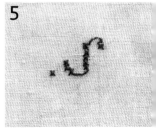

4

Remove warp threads.

5

If needed layer cloth over the top and press with an iron to flatten.

A Scandinavian Cityscape

he color codes used throughout this book refer to Cosmo
rand embroidery floss. Equivalent codes for DMC floss are
iven in a chart found inside the back cover of this book.

※Unless otherwise specified, use two strands

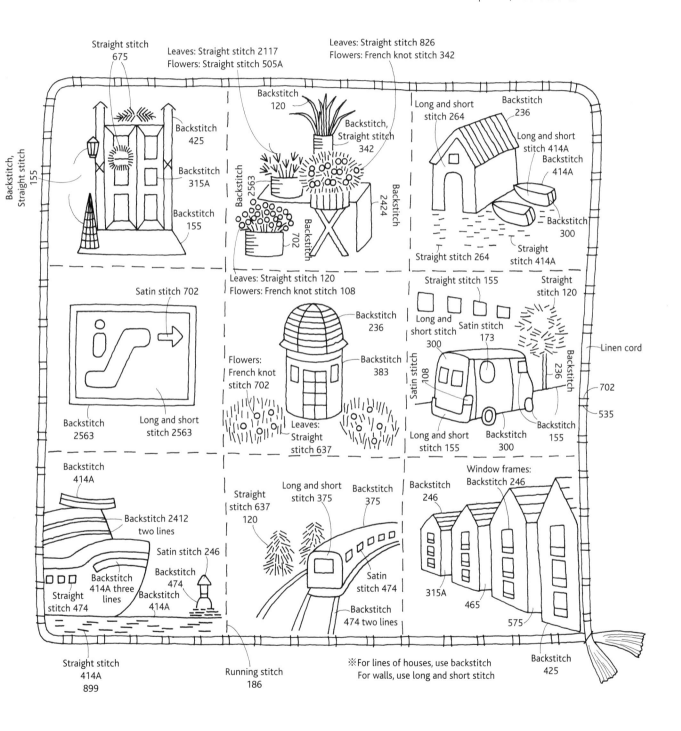

Straight stitch
675

Leaves: Straight stitch 2117
Flowers: Straight stitch 505A

Leaves: Straight stitch 826
Flowers: French knot stitch 342

Backstitch
120

Backstitch
425

Backstitch,
Straight stitch
342

Backstitch
315A

Backstitch
155

Backstitch,
Straight stitch
155

Backstitch
2563

Backstitch
702

Backstitch
2424

Long and short
stitch 264

Backstitch
236

Long and short
stitch 414A

Backstitch
414A

Backstitch
300

Straight stitch 264

Straight
stitch 414A

Satin stitch 702

Leaves: Straight stitch 120
Flowers: French knot stitch 108

Backstitch
2563

Long and short
stitch 2563

Flowers:
French knot
stitch 702

Backstitch
236

Backstitch
383

Leaves:
Straight
stitch 637

Straight stitch 155

Straight
stitch 120

Long and
short stitch
300

Satin stitch
173

Backstitch
236

Linen cord

Satin stitch
108

Long and short
stitch 155

Backstitch
300

Backstitch
155

702

535

Backstitch
414A

Backstitch 2412
two lines

Satin stitch 246

Straight
stitch 474

Backstitch
414A three
lines

Backstitch
474
Backstitch
414A

Straight
stitch 637
120

Long and short
stitch 375

Backstitch
375

Satin
stitch 474

Backstitch
474 two lines

Window frames:
Backstitch 246

Backstitch
246

Backstitch 246

315A

465

575

Backstitch
425

Straight stitch
414A
899

Running stitch
186

※For lines of houses, use backstitch
For walls, use long and short stitch

Cute Cups

The color codes used throughout this book refer to Cosmo brand embroidery floss. Equivalent codes for DMC floss are given in a chart found inside the back cover of this book.

※Use two strands unless otherwise specified

Backstitch 312

※Use straight stitch for nose and mouth 312

Backstitch 894

Join fabric here

Backstitch 129 (use one strand)

Backstitch 477

Backstitch 403 (use three strands)

Backstitch 895

Backstitch 654

Satin stitch 413

Backstitch 632 (use one strand)

Long and short stitch 654

Backstitch 310

Backstitch 328

Long and short stitch 310

Seed stitch 328

Long and short stitch 252

Backstitch 600

Satin stitch 525

Satin stitch 215

Satin stitch 892

Satin stitch 665

Backstitch 665

Backstitch 600

Satin stitch 312

Backstitch 215

French knot stitch 215 (use one strand)

Backstitch 21 (use one stran

Satin stitch 714

Backstitch 312

Backstitch 477

Satin stitch 302

Satin stitch 577

Backstitch 328

Backstitch 895

Satin stitch 386

Straight stitch 895

Backstitch 773

Backstitch 895

Satin stitch 215

Backstitch 215

Backstitch 2311

Long and short stitch 2311

Backstitch 894

Satin stitch 600

Long and short stitch 894

Satin stitch 892

Backstitch 242

Backstitch 600

Satin stitch 310

Satin stitch 186

Backstitch 368

Backstitch 328

Straight stitch 368

Satin stitch 328

Backstitch 328 (use one strand)

Backstitch 242 (use one strand)

French knot stitch 242 (use one strand)

51

A Cosy Room

※Use two strands unless otherwise specified
※Use long and short stitch unless otherwise specified

The color codes used throughout this book refer to Cosmo brand embroidery floss. Equivalent codes for DMC floss are given in a chart found inside the back cover of this book.

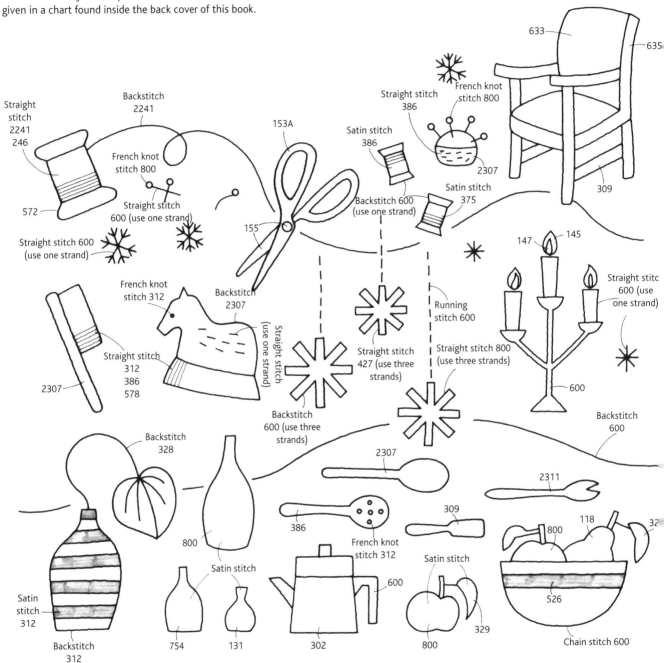

Straight stitch 2241 246

Backstitch 2241

French knot stitch 800

Straight stitch 600 (use one strand)

Straight stitch 600 (use one strand)

572

153A

Satin stitch 386

Straight stitch 386

French knot stitch 800

2307

Satin stitch 375

Backstitch 600 (use one strand)

633

635

309

155

Backstitch 2307

Straight stitch (use one strand)

Backstitch 600 (use three strands)

Straight stitch 427 (use three strands)

Running stitch 600

Straight stitch 800 (use three strands)

147   145

Straight stitch 600 (use one strand)

600

French knot stitch 312

Straight stitch 312 386 578

2307

Backstitch 328

Backstitch 600

800

Satin stitch

386

French knot stitch 312

600

Satin stitch

309

2307

2311

800

118

32

526

Satin stitch 312

Backstitch 312

754   131

302

Satin stitch

800   329

Chain stitch 600

Backstitch 600

325A

600

Straight stitch 152A

Backstitch 600

578 600

Backstitch 600

302

Straight stitch 152A

Backstitch 600

118

2311

242

600

506

Backstitch 600

404

Backstitch 2241

Backstitch 309

309

346

French knot stitch 312

Backstitch 346

2214

French knot stitch 346

214

Backstitch 214

Backstitch 600

Backstitch 600

405

2214

800

325A

302

Backstitch 800

800

309

Backstitch 600

Backstitch 600

French knot stitch 800

Backstitch 600

Backstitch 600

Backstitch 118

Backstitch 600

118

Backstitch 600

800

Satin stitch 2214

302

152A

118

A Tidy Kitchen

※For lines, use two strands and sew backstitch
※Use two strands unless otherwise specified

The color codes used throughout this book refer to Cosmo brand embroidery floss. Equivalent codes for DMC floss are given in a chart found inside the back cover of this book.

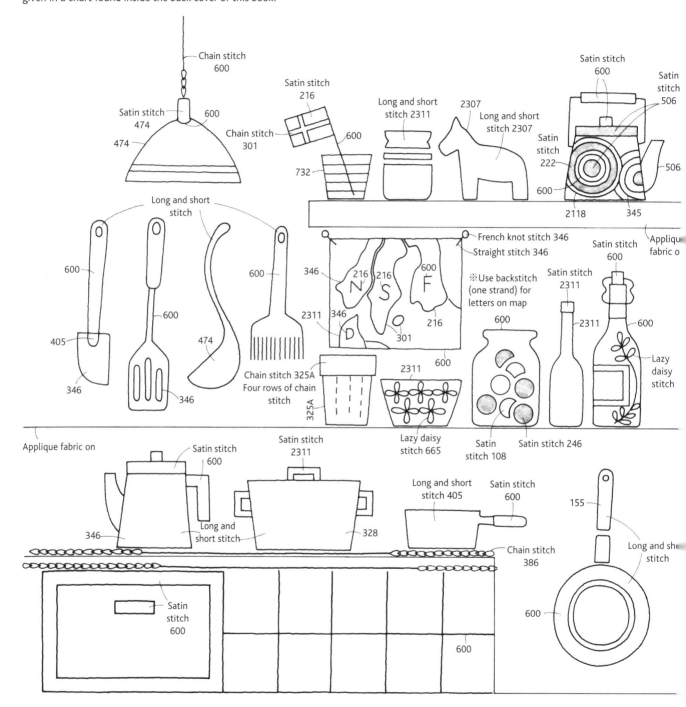

Chain stitch 600

Satin stitch 474

474   600

Satin stitch 216

Chain stitch 301

600

732

Long and short stitch 2311

2307

Long and short stitch 2307

Satin stitch 600

Satin stitch 506

Satin stitch 222

600

506

2118   345

Applique fabric o

Long and short stitch

600

600

405

346

474

600

346

2311

346

346   216   216   600   F

N   S

D   301   216

600

French knot stitch 346

Straight stitch 346

※Use backstitch (one strand) for letters on map

Satin stitch 600

Satin stitch 2311

2311

600

Lazy daisy stitch

Chain stitch 325A
Four rows of chain stitch

325A

2311

Lazy daisy stitch 665

600

Satin stitch 108

Satin stitch 246

Applique fabric on

Satin stitch 600

Satin stitch 2311

346

Long and short stitch

328

Long and short stitch 405

Satin stitch 600

Chain stitch 386

155

Long and she stitch

600

Satin stitch 600

600

54

Satin stitch 329

Long and short stitch 2311

367

813

Satin stitch 326 329

474

Satin stitch 506

311

216

Satin stitch 329

Satin stitch 665

346

Satin stitch 2118

Straight stitch 329

Running stitch 813

Satin stitch 474

Satin stitch 311

600

Long and short stitch 216

Long and short stitch 858

Outline stitch 213

Satin stitch 311

307

2307

305

Backstitch 600 (one strand)

Smooth

Backstitch 600 (one strand)

600

346

216

KNÄCKE BRÖD

Backstitch 600 (one strand)

Satin stitch 217

311

Satin stitch 213

French knot stitch 405

KAFFE MJÖLK

216

311

600

Satin stitch 600

600

301

Outline stitch 301

217

252

329

Satin stitch 311

311

311

Satin stitch 222

choklad dryck

Backstitch 312 (one strand)

405

Satin stitch 311 311

345

Satin stitch

Backstitch 301 (one strand)

523

600

Long and short stitch

Long and short stitch

702

Herringbone stitch 311

Long and short stitch 312 (one strand)

Backstitch 600 (one strand)

korvapuusti

600

Satin stitch

Straight stitch 2118

2118

Satin stitch 500

253

Satin stitch

311

Running stitch 345

Outline stitch 309

523

Outline stitch 306

Backstitch 253

A Visit to the Flea Market

Unless specified, backstitch is used for outlines.
Fill in areas using long and short stitch (two strands)

The color codes used throughout this book refer to Cosmo brand embroidery floss. Equivalent codes for DMC floss are given in a chart found inside the back cover of this book.

Backstitch 600

Satin stitch 119

346

600

Satin stitch 600

Satin stitch 318

Running stitch 600

Satin stitch 119

Satin stitch 121

2307 (one strand)

578

2311

Satin stitch 600

Antiikki

Satin stitch 308 (one strand)

218

287

665

600

※Use satin stitch for fruit (one strand)

Satin stitch 2118 (one strand)

600

Satin stitch 525 (one strand)

Satin stitch 600 and French knot stitch 100 (one strand)

600

168

Lazy daisy stitch, from center out: 556, 665, 664A

Satin stitch 302 (one strand)

600 (one strand)

PiRKKA

346

Kasvirasvasekoite

633

Satin stitch 346

633 (one strand)

600

892

891

891

893

892

891

Satin stitch 892

Satin stitch 895

Satin stitch 600 (one strand)

Satin stitch 311

600

Satin stitch 2307

Satin stitch 213

2311

Satin stitch

Satin stitch

310

600 764

766

715
(one strand)

404

100

Back stitch
712

※All satin stitch

713
(one strand)

214

2214

※All satin stitch

600

Satin stitch
307

Satin stitch
2118

Satin stitch
120

600

Chain stitch
346

344

atin
itch
(one
and)

406 600

13

French knot
stitch 312

※Use French knot stitch for eyes 600

188

895

413

600

100 2120

312

413

2129

Satin
stitch

312

Straight
stitch 312
(one strand)

309 Satin
stitch

French knot
stitch 346

312

Chain stitch
100

Satin stitch

310

312

310

312

Chain stitch 467

308

2307

Hallo

Use one strand for letters

600

120

Satin stitch 346

2307

255

800

Satin stitch 574

577

600

Use french knot stitch for seeds 600 (one strand)

Scandinavian Forest Designs

※Unless otherwise specified, use long and short stitch (two strands)
※Use French knot stitch for eyes
※Use backstitch for lines (two strands)

Backstitch 320

Straight stitch 320

Backstitch 309

Satin stitch 100

307

2307

309

309

129
147
145
1000
309
703
131
Straight stitch 600
Satin stitch 346
312
Straight stitch 311
120
118
309

703
858
706
2311
309
Straight stitch 309

376
858
1000
703
309
312
Straight stitch 312

Straight stitch 100 (four strands)

858
406
188
703
French knot stitch 100

Backstitch 121
Straight stitch 121
2311
255
255
253
167
French knot stitch 100

Straight stitch 311
309

188
2311

Straight stitch 320
Backstitch 320
Backstitch 309

Backstitch 320
Straight stitch 311
308
311
Backstitch 600
Satin stitch 858
600
Backstitch 655 (three strands)
634
Straight stitch 120

145
147
312
346
Straight stitch 312
Backstitch 312

Backstitch 320
Straight stitch 320
Backstitch 309

169
320
308
255
166
255
119
320
308
169
119
310
308
French knot stitch 100

The color codes used throughout this book refer to Cosmo brand embroidery floss. Equivalent codes for DMC floss are given in chart found inside the back cover of this bo

58

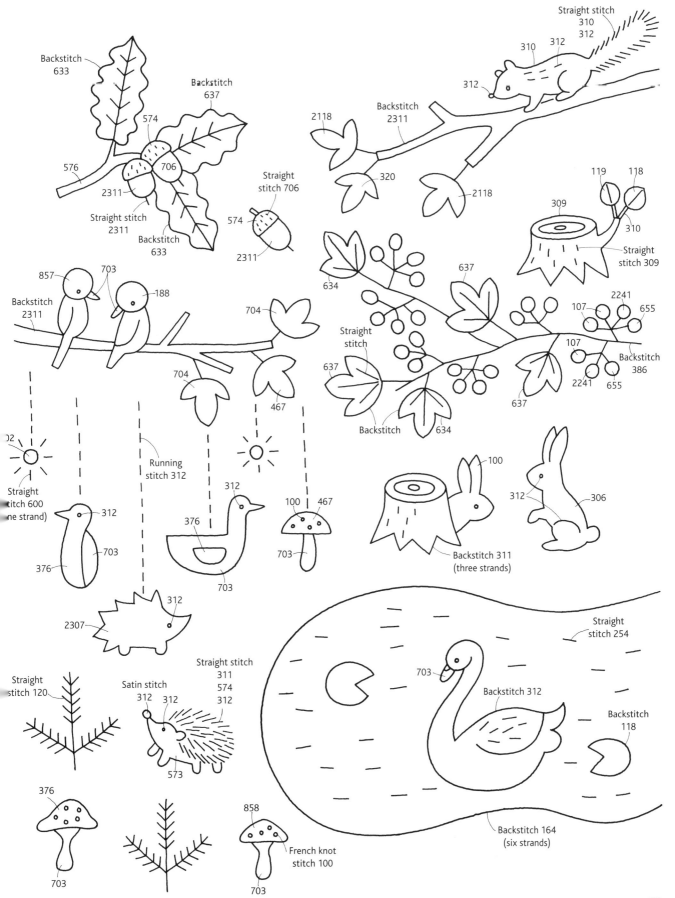

Backstitch 633

Backstitch 637

574

706

576

2311

Straight stitch 2311

Backstitch 633

Straight stitch 706

574

2311

Straight stitch 310 312

310

312

312

Backstitch 2311

2118

320

2118

119 118

309

310

Straight stitch 309

857 703

Backstitch 2311

188

704

704

467

637

634

Straight stitch

637

Backstitch 637 634

637

107 2241

107 655

2241 655

Backstitch 386

02

Straight stitch 600 (one strand)

Running stitch 312

312

376

100 467

703

312

703

376

100

Backstitch 311 (three strands)

312

306

2307

312

Straight stitch 254

703

Backstitch 312

Backstitch 118

Straight stitch 120

Satin stitch 312 312

Straight stitch 311 574 312

573

376

858

French knot stitch 100

Backstitch 164 (six strands)

703

703

The color codes used throughout this book refer to Cosmo brand embroidery floss. Equivalent codes for DMC floss are given in a chart found inside the back cover of this book.

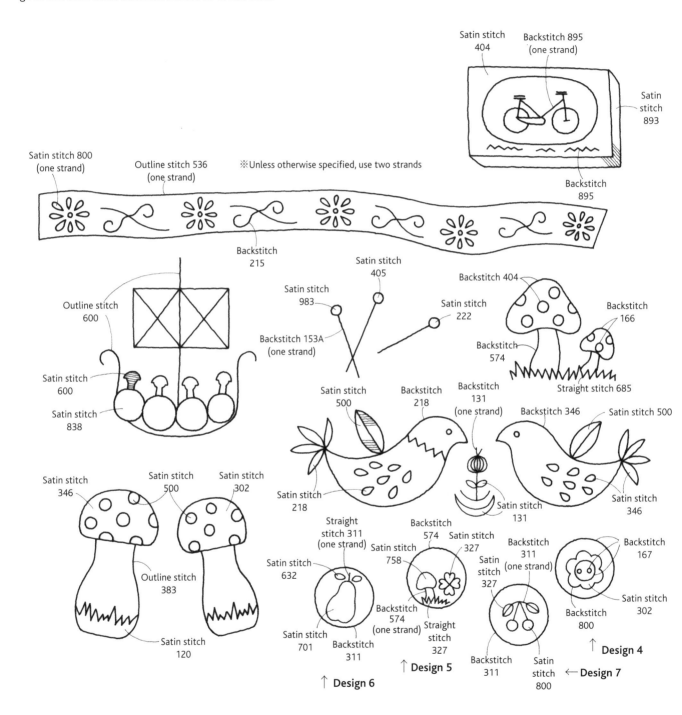

Satin stitch 404
Backstitch 895 (one strand)
Satin stitch 893
Backstitch 895

Satin stitch 800 (one strand)
Outline stitch 536 (one strand)
※Unless otherwise specified, use two strands
Backstitch 215

Outline stitch 600
Satin stitch 600
Satin stitch 838

Satin stitch 983
Backstitch 153A (one strand)
Satin stitch 405
Satin stitch 222

Backstitch 404
Backstitch 166
Backstitch 574
Straight stitch 685

Satin stitch 500
Backstitch 218
Backstitch 131 (one strand)
Backstitch 346
Satin stitch 500
Satin stitch 218
Satin stitch 131
Satin stitch 346

Satin stitch 346
Satin stitch 500
Satin stitch 302
Outline stitch 383
Satin stitch 120

Straight stitch 311 (one strand)
Satin stitch 632
Satin stitch 701
Backstitch 311
↑ Design 6

Backstitch 574
Satin stitch 758
Backstitch 574 (one strand)
Satin stitch 327
Straight stitch 327
↑ Design 5

Satin stitch 327
Backstitch 311 (one strand)
Backstitch 311
Satin stitch 800
← Design 7

Backstitch 167
Backstitch 800
Satin stitch 302
↑ Design 4

60

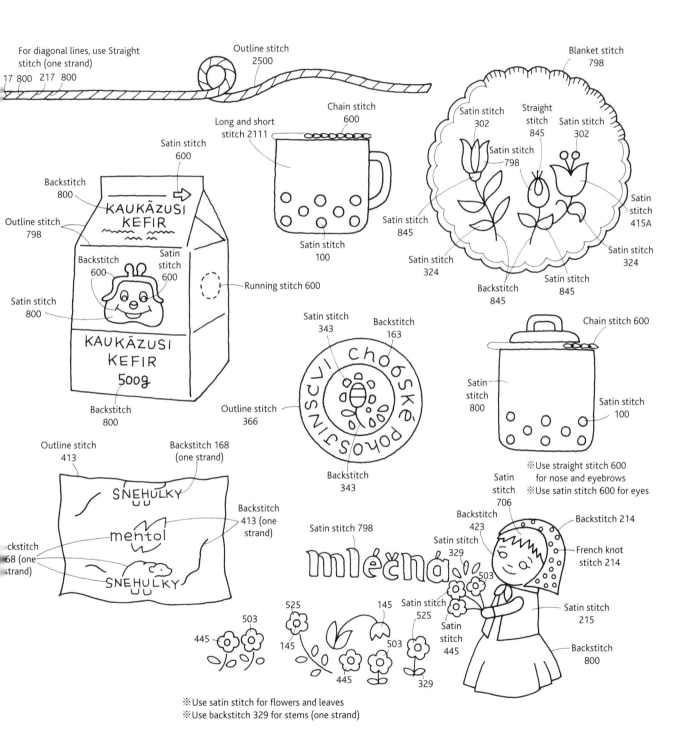

For diagonal lines, use Straight stitch (one strand)
17 800 217 800

Outline stitch 2500

Chain stitch 600

Blanket stitch 798

Satin stitch 302   Straight stitch 845   Satin stitch 302

Satin stitch 798

Satin stitch 415A

Long and short stitch 2111

Satin stitch 600

Backstitch 800

Outline stitch 798

Backstitch 600   Satin stitch 600

Satin stitch 800

KAUKÁZUSI KEFIR

Running stitch 600

Satin stitch 845

Satin stitch 324

Backstitch 845

Satin stitch 845

Satin stitch 324

KAUKÁZUSI KEFIR 500g

Backstitch 800

Satin stitch 343   Backstitch 163

Outline stitch 366

choóské pohoSinSCLI

Backstitch 343

Chain stitch 600

Satin stitch 800

Satin stitch 100

Outline stitch 413   Backstitch 168 (one strand)

Backstitch 413 (one strand)

SNEHULKY

mentol

SNEHULKY

ckstitch 68 (one strand)

※Use straight stitch 600 for nose and eyebrows
※Use satin stitch 600 for eyes

Satin stitch 706

Backstitch 423

Satin stitch 329

Backstitch 214

French knot stitch 214

Satin stitch 798

mléčná

503

Satin stitch 215

Satin stitch 525

Satin stitch 445

Backstitch 800

503
445   525   145   503   Satin stitch 525
145   445   329

※Use satin stitch for flowers and leaves
※Use backstitch 329 for stems (one strand)

61

The Music's Playing

※Unless otherwise specified, use backstitch (one strand)
※For faces, use 312. Use straight stitch for eyes and mouths
※Use satin stitch 835 for cheeks

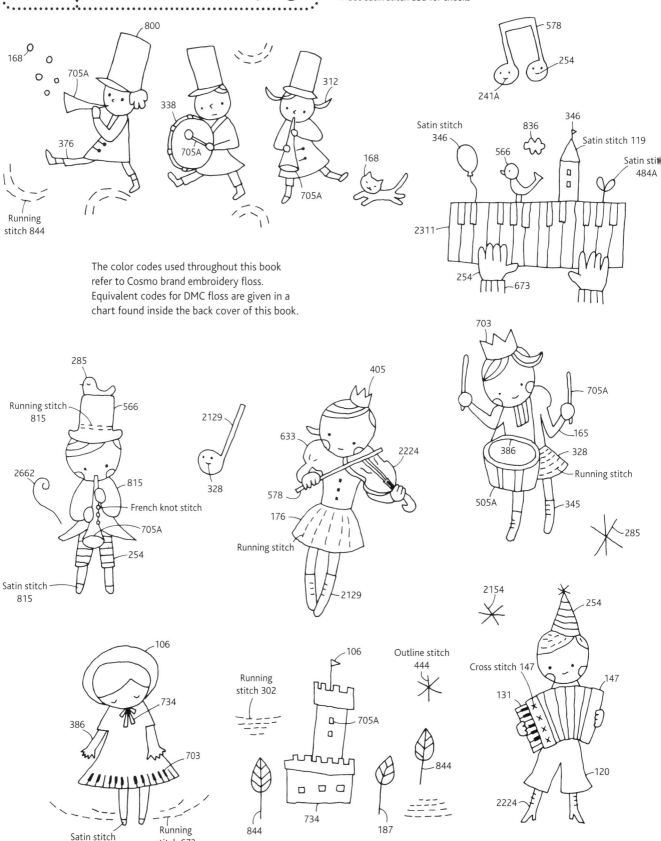

168
800
705A
376
338
705A
312
168
705A
Running stitch 844

578
254
241A

Satin stitch 346
346
836
566
Satin stitch 119
Satin stitch 484A
2311
254
673

The color codes used throughout this book refer to Cosmo brand embroidery floss. Equivalent codes for DMC floss are given in a chart found inside the back cover of this book.

285
Running stitch 815
566
2662
815
French knot stitch
705A
254
Satin stitch 815

2129
328

405
633
2224
578
176
Running stitch
2129

703
705A
165
386
328
505A
345
Running stitch
285

2154
254
Cross stitch 147
131
147
2224
120

106
734
386
703
Satin stitch 106
Running stitch 673

Running stitch 302
106
705A
734

Outline stitch 444
844

844
187

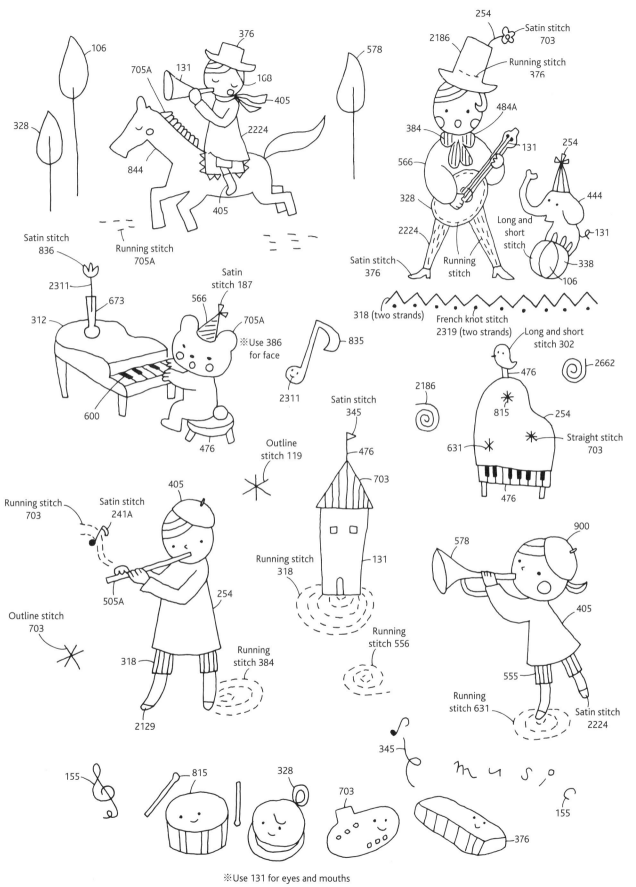

106

328

376

705A

131

168

405

844

2224

578

254

Satin stitch 703

2186

Running stitch 376

384

484A

131

566

328

254

2224

444

Long and short stitch

131

338

106

Satin stitch 376

Running stitch

318 (two strands)

French knot stitch 2319 (two strands)

Long and short stitch 302

Satin stitch 836

2311

673

312

Satin stitch 187

566

705A

※Use 386 for face

835

2311

Satin stitch 345

2186

476

2662

815

254

600

476

Straight stitch 703

631

476

476

Outline stitch 119

Running stitch 703

Satin stitch 241A

405

476

703

900

578

Outline stitch 703

505A

254

131

555

405

318

Running stitch 318

Running stitch 384

Running stitch 556

Running stitch 631

Satin stitch 2224

2129

345

155

815

328

703

155

376

※Use 131 for eyes and mouths

I Love Fruit!

※Unless otherwise specified, use backstitch (one strand)
※Unless otherwise specified, use 312 for faces and straight stitch for eyes and mouths
※Use satin stitch 835 for cheeks

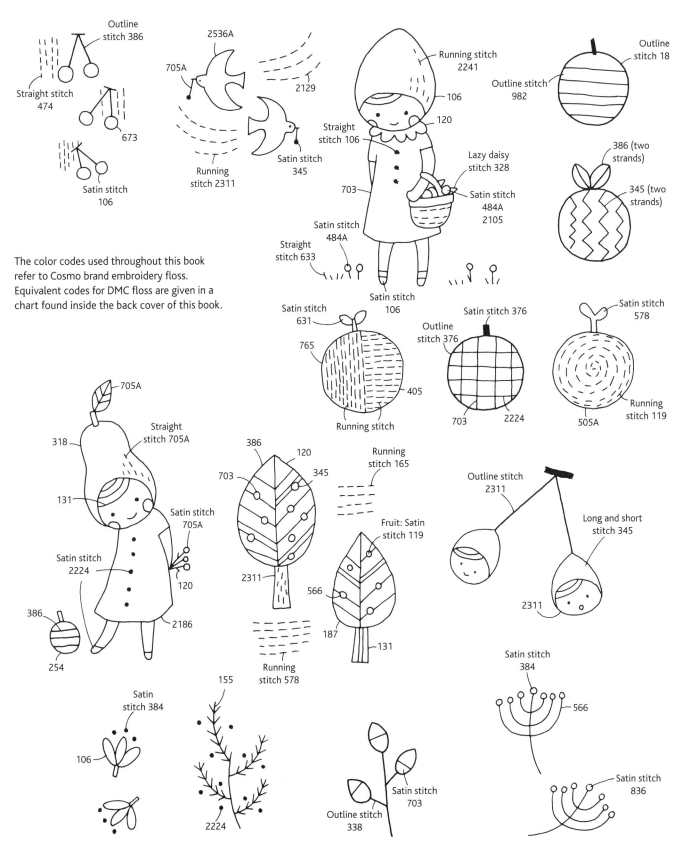

Outline stitch 386

Straight stitch 474

673

Satin stitch 106

2536A

705A

2129

Running stitch 2311

Satin stitch 345

Running stitch 2241

106

120

Straight stitch 106

703

Lazy daisy stitch 328

Satin stitch 484A 2105

Satin stitch 484A

Straight stitch 633

Satin stitch 106

Outline stitch 18

Outline stitch 982

386 (two strands)

345 (two strands)

Satin stitch 631

765

405

Running stitch

Satin stitch 376

Outline stitch 376

703

2224

Satin stitch 578

505A

Running stitch 119

The color codes used throughout this book refer to Cosmo brand embroidery floss. Equivalent codes for DMC floss are given in a chart found inside the back cover of this book.

705A

318

131

Straight stitch 705A

Satin stitch 705A

Satin stitch 2224

120

2186

386

254

386

703

120

345

2311

Running stitch 165

Fruit: Satin stitch 119

566

187

131

Running stitch 578

Outline stitch 2311

Long and short stitch 345

2311

Satin stitch 384

566

Satin stitch 384

106

155

2224

Satin stitch 703

Outline stitch 338

Satin stitch 836

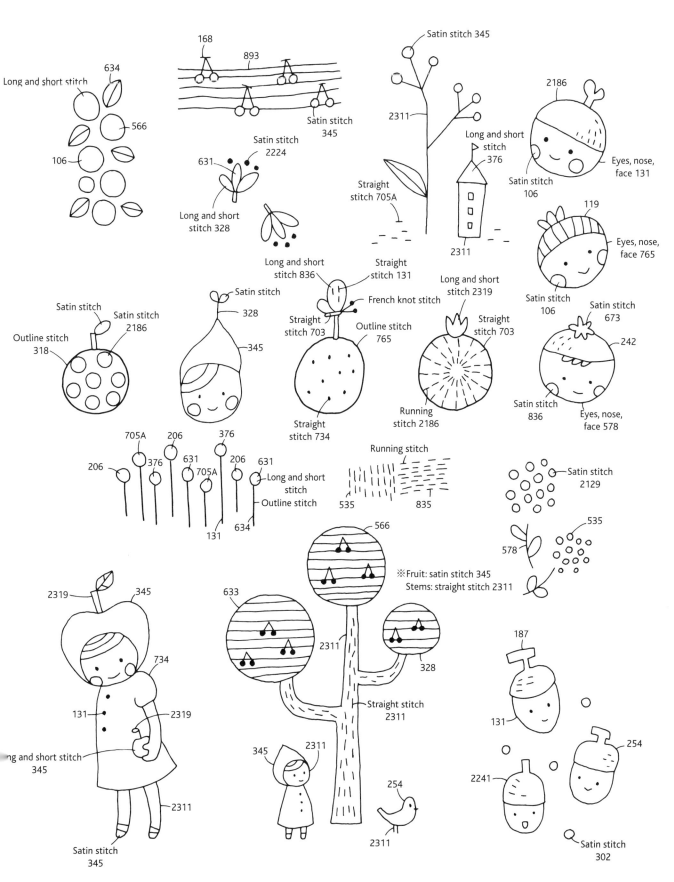

Long and short stitch

634

566

106

168

893

Satin stitch 345

Satin stitch 2224

631

Long and short stitch 328

Satin stitch 345

Straight stitch 705A

2311

Long and short stitch 376

Satin stitch 106

2311

2186

Eyes, nose, face 131

119

Eyes, nose, face 765

Satin stitch 106

Satin stitch 673

242

Satin stitch 836

Eyes, nose, face 578

Satin stitch

Outline stitch 318

Satin stitch 2186

Satin stitch 328

345

Long and short stitch 836

Straight stitch 131

French knot stitch

Straight stitch 703

Outline stitch 765

Long and short stitch 2319

Straight stitch 703

Straight stitch 734

Running stitch 2186

705A

206

376

206

376

631

705A

206

631

131

634

Long and short stitch

Outline stitch

Running stitch

535

835

Satin stitch 2129

578

535

※Fruit: satin stitch 345
Stems: straight stitch 2311

2319

345

734

131

2319

ng and short stitch 345

2311

Satin stitch 345

566

633

2311

328

Straight stitch 2311

345

2311

254

2311

187

131

254

2241

Satin stitch 302

65

French knot stitch 836: six strands

※Unless otherwise specified, use two strands

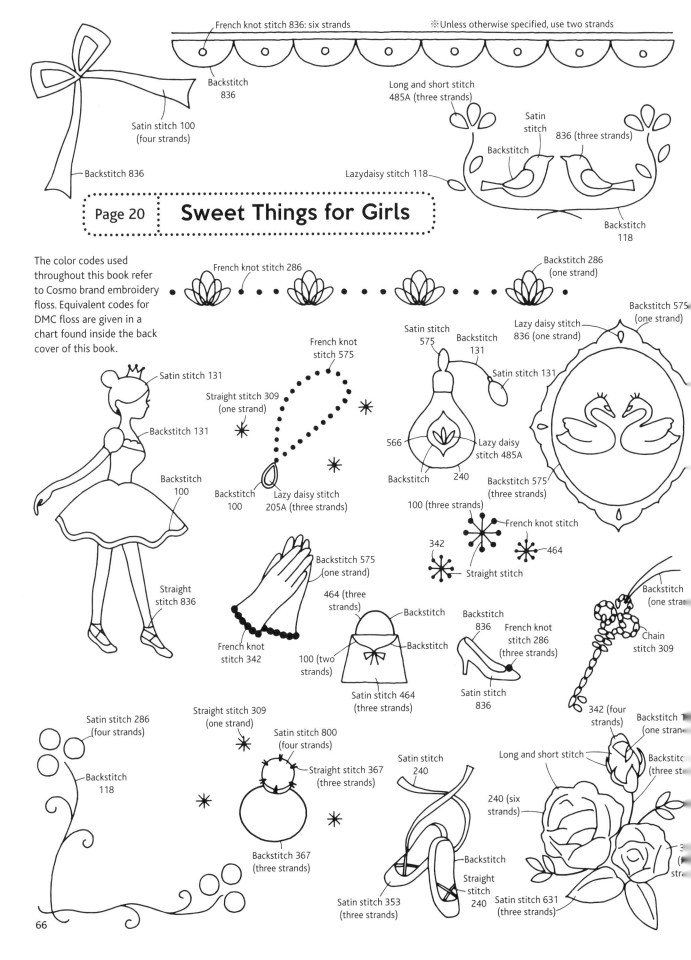

Backstitch 836

Satin stitch 100
(four strands)

Backstitch 836

Long and short stitch
485A (three strands)

Satin stitch

836 (three strands)

Backstitch

Lazydaisy stitch 118

Backstitch 118

Page 20 : **Sweet Things for Girls**

The color codes used throughout this book refer to Cosmo brand embroidery floss. Equivalent codes for DMC floss are given in a chart found inside the back cover of this book.

French knot stitch 286

Backstitch 286
(one strand)

Backstitch 575
(one strand)

French knot
stitch 575

Satin stitch 131

Backstitch 131

Straight stitch 309
(one strand)

Satin stitch
575

Backstitch
131

Satin stitch 131

Lazy daisy stitch
836 (one strand)

Backstitch
100

Backstitch
100

Lazy daisy stitch
205A (three strands)

566

Lazy daisy
stitch 485A

Backstitch   240

Backstitch 575
(three strands)

100 (three strands)

French knot stitch

342

464

Straight stitch

Backstitch 575
(one strand)

464 (three
strands)

Backstitch

Backstitch

Backstitch
836

French knot
stitch 286
(three strands)

Backstitch
(one stran

Chain
stitch 309

French knot
stitch 342

100 (two
strands)

Satin stitch 464
(three strands)

Satin stitch
836

342 (four
strands)

Backstitch 1
(one stran

Straight
stitch 836

Satin stitch 286
(four strands)

Backstitch
118

Straight stitch 309
(one strand)

Satin stitch 800
(four strands)

Straight stitch 367
(three strands)

Satin stitch
240

Long and short stitch

Backstitch
(three st

240 (six
strands)

Backstitch 367
(three strands)

Backstitch

Straight
stitch
240

Satin stitch 353
(three strands)

Satin stitch 631
(three strands)

66

Lazy daisy stitch 836

French knot stitch 836

Backstitch

836 (three strands)

Backstitch 836 (three strands)

Backstitch 575 (one strand)

tin stitch 485A

Satin stitch 575 (four strands)

575

Backstitch

Backstitch 631

zy daisy itch 631

836

566

French knot stitch 836 (three strands)

Straight stitch 105

Backstitch 131

Straight stitch

Lazy daisy stitch 118

Backstitch 575

Satin stitch

Backstitch

464

Satin stitch 105

Satin stitch 836 (three strands)

Lazy daisy stitch 119

Backstitch

Satin stitch 464

Backstitch 464

Backstitch

Satin stitch 374 (three strands)

Lazy daisy stitch

French knot stitch

Chain stitch

Chain stitch

※Use 575 for mirror

Satin stitch 800 (three strands)

Satin stitch 131

Backstitch 309 (three strands)

Backstitch 119

Backstitch 131 (one strand)

Backstitch

Backstitch 168 (six strands)

Satin stitch 309 (three strands)

※Use 575 for bag

Backstitch 462 (four lines)

French knot stitch 462

100

240

342

Backstitch 119 (one strand)

Long and short stitch

Backstitch

Backstitch 631

Satin stitch 631

Satin stitch 631

Backstitch 631

Satin stitch 309

Lazy daisy stitch 836 (one strand)

Satin stitch 566 (three strands)

Backstitch 566 (three strands)

Satin stitch 374 (three strands)

Backstitch 309 (three strands)

Backstitch 631 (one strand)

Backstitch 425 (three strands)

Backstitch 404 (four strands)

French knot stitch 131 (three strands)

Satin stitch 131 (three strands)

Satin stitch 404 (four strands)

Chain stitch 309 (three strands)

100

Lazy daisy stitch 836 (three strands)

stitch (three nds)

Satin stitch 309 (three strands)

Chain stitch 425 (three strands)

Backstitch 631 (three strands)

67

Strips and Polka Dots

Please see inside back cover for a chart converting Cosmo brand floss to DMC brand.

Satin stitch 2212
893
※Use satin stitch for cherries
164
857
2262
2212
Applique fabric on
2343
857
893
702
326
503
522
857
310
2262
556
702
855
318
164
2343
475
857
Running stitch 311
503
French knot stitch
857
556
503
146
Applique fabric on
857
342
857
Satin stitch 311
French knot stitch
857
Satin stitch 146
342
Satin stitch 2307
475
857
2343
342
2343
2343
556
2262
Satin stitch 733
302
893
475
※Make stripes in 893 and 302 for bees
893
523
346
503
854
326
Satin stitch 573
310
146
310
506
893
893
857
733
Long and short stitch 385
164
702
702
328
855
※Use 893 for eyes and nose
106
Satin stitch 185
857
French knot stitch
Satin stitch 522
556
2262

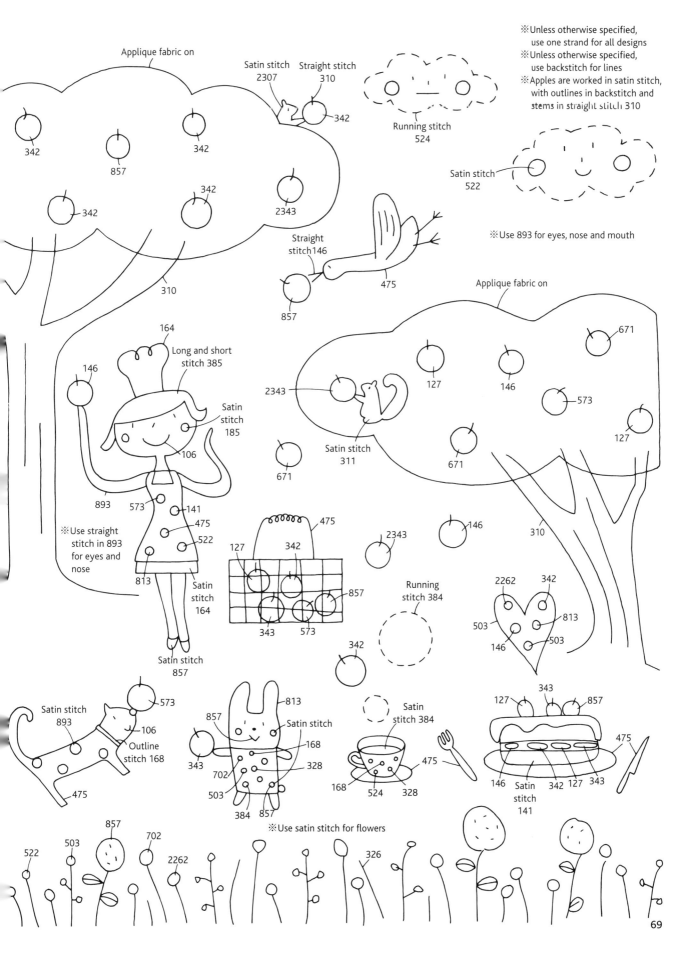

Applique fabric on

Satin stitch 2307　Straight stitch 310

342

342

857

342

342

342

2343

310

Running stitch 524

Satin stitch 522

※Unless otherwise specified, use one strand for all designs
※Unless otherwise specified, use backstitch for lines
※Apples are worked in satin stitch, with outlines in backstitch and stems in straight stitch 310

Straight stitch 146

475

857

※Use 893 for eyes, nose and mouth

Applique fabric on

671

164

Long and short stitch 385

146

Satin stitch 185

106

2343

127

146

573

127

Satin stitch 311

671

671

310

893　573

141

475

522

※Use straight stitch in 893 for eyes and nose

813

Satin stitch 164

Satin stitch 857

127　342

475

857

343　573

2343

146

Running stitch 384

2262　342

503

813

503

146

342

343　857

573

Satin stitch 893

106

Outline stitch 168

813

857

Satin stitch

168

328

703

503

384　857

Satin stitch 384

475

168　524　328

127

146　Satin stitch 141　342　127　343

475

475

857

702

2262

326

522　503

※Use satin stitch for flowers

Please see inside back cover for a chart converting Cosmo brand floss to DMC brand.

※Unless otherwise specified, use backstitch (two strands)

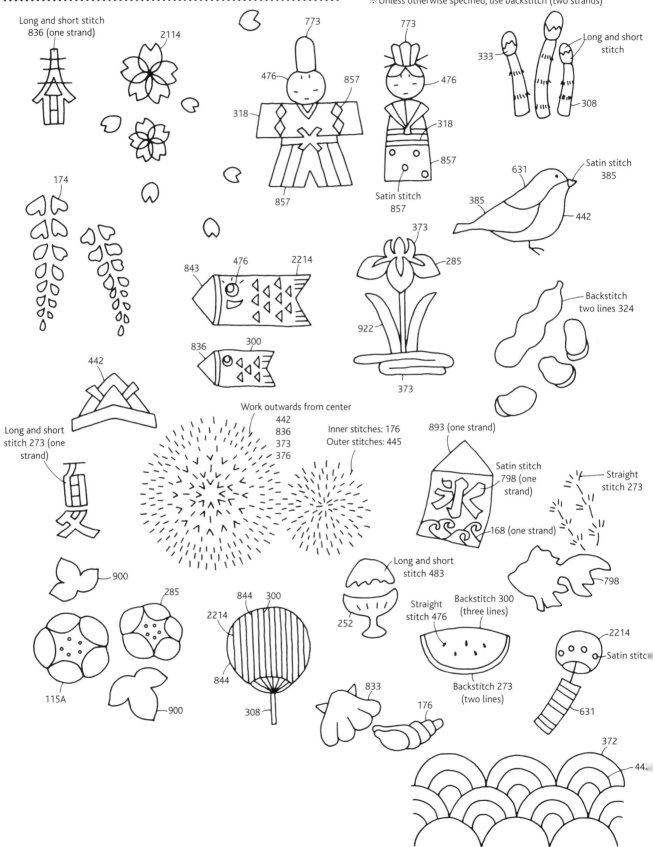

Long and short stitch 836 (one strand)

2114

773

773

Long and short stitch

333

308

476

857

318

857

476

318

857

Satin stitch 857

174

631

Satin stitch 385

385

442

843

476

2214

373

285

Backstitch two lines 324

836

300

922

373

442

Long and short stitch 273 (one strand)

Work outwards from center
442
836
373
376

Inner stitches: 176
Outer stitches: 445

893 (one strand)

Satin stitch 798 (one strand)

168 (one strand)

Straight stitch 273

798

900

Long and short stitch 483

285

844

300

Straight stitch 476

Backstitch 300 (three lines)

2214

2214

Satin stitc

844

252

115A

900

308

833

176

Backstitch 273 (two lines)

631

372

442

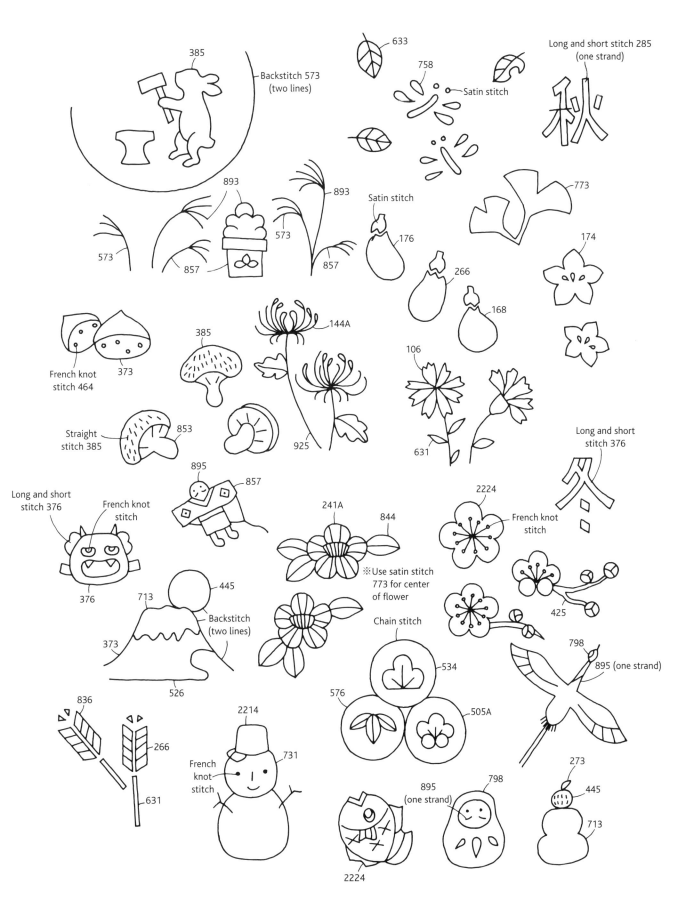

385

Backstitch 573
(two lines)

633

758

Satin stitch

Long and short stitch 285
(one strand)

秋

893

893

573

573

857

857

Satin stitch

176

266

168

773

174

French knot
stitch 464

373

385

144A

925

106

631

Long and short
stitch 376

Straight
stitch 385

853

Long and short
stitch 376

French knot
stitch

376

895

857

241A

844

※Use satin stitch
773 for center
of flower

2224

French knot
stitch

冬

425

713

445

Backstitch
(two lines)

373

526

Chain stitch

534

576

505A

798

895 (one strand)

836

266

631

2214

French
knot
stitch

731

895
(one strand)

798

273

445

713

2224

Birds & Flowers

The color codes used throughout this book refer to Cosmo brand embroidery floss. Equivalent codes for DMC floss are given in a chart found inside the back cover of this book.

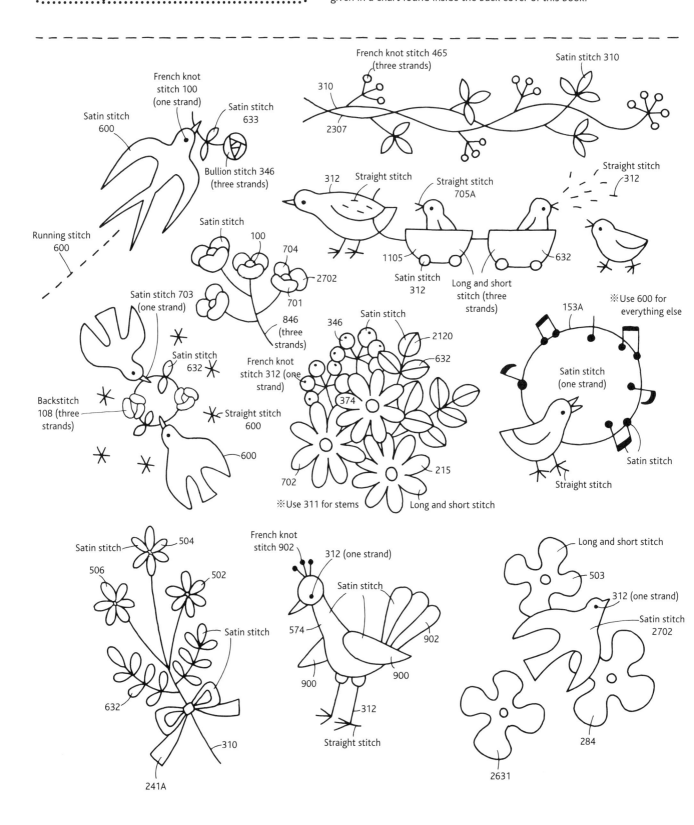

French knot stitch 100 (one strand)

Satin stitch 600

Satin stitch 633

Bullion stitch 346 (three strands)

French knot stitch 465 (three strands)

Satin stitch 310

310

2307

Running stitch 600

Satin stitch

Satin stitch 703 (one strand)

100

704

2702

701

846 (three strands)

French knot stitch 312 (one strand)

Satin stitch 632

Backstitch 108 (three strands)

Straight stitch 600

600

312

Straight stitch

Straight stitch 705A

Straight stitch 312

1105

Satin stitch 312

Long and short stitch (three strands)

632

346

Satin stitch

2120

632

374

702

※Use 311 for stems

215

Long and short stitch

153A

※Use 600 for everything else

Satin stitch (one strand)

Satin stitch

Straight stitch

Satin stitch 504

Satin stitch

506

502

Satin stitch

632

310

241A

French knot stitch 902

312 (one strand)

Satin stitch

574

900

900

312

Straight stitch

Long and short stitch

503

312 (one strand)

Satin stitch 2702

284

2631

72

※Unless otherwise specified, use two strands ※Use French knot stitch for eyes (one strand)
※Lines are worked in backstitch

Running stitch 600

French knot stitch 1105

702 Long and short stitch

Straight stitch 600 (one strand)

Satin stitch 1105

Satin stitch 312

Satin stitch 600

Satin stitch (three strands)

483

486

French knot stitch 100

600

Satin stitch 346

120

312

French knot stitch 1105

894

Satin stitch

Satin stitch 120

312

484A

846

600

326

2154

600 (three strands)

Straight stitch

600

Satin stitch 2702

467

French knot stitch

465

465

462

Straight stitch

Satin stitch 312

312

312

Satin stitch 858

Straight stitch

600

312

Satin stitch 633

2631

Long and short stitch 701

2118

893

120

Lazy daisy stitch (four strands)

Fill in branch using outline stitch 311

Satin stitch 1105

2631

French knot stitch 311 (one strand)

Satin stitch 2241

Straight stitch 311

Satin stitch 263

633

※Use 312 for eye (three strands)

632

Straight stitch

107

311

French knot stitch (Wind thread loosely around needle and secure without crushing the loop)

French knot stitch 100

French knot stitch 186

119

Satin stitch 703

310

Satin stitch

575

312

Satin stitch 2307

121

119

2311

702

Satin stitch 384

308

Long and short stitch

2307

Straight stitch 312

Tasty Tea Time

The color codes used throughout this book refer to Cosmo brand embroidery floss. Equivalent codes for DMC floss are given in a chart found inside the back cover of this book.

※Use french knot stitch 312 for eyes and noses (two strands)

Straight stitch 312
152A
Satin stitch
703
800
TEA TIME!!
French knot stitch 312
Straight stitch 600
Satin stitch 600
Backstitch 633
French knot stitch 703
Satin stitch 506

Satin stitch 346
Long and short stitch 118
Satin stitch 152A
Satin stitch 2212
2563
Satin stitch 701
105
631
French knot stitch 310
Backstitch 310
Satin stitch 309
French knot stitch 302 (three strands)
Straight stitch 2120

Satin stitch 312
702
Satin stitch 310
309
902
Long and short stitch
Satin stitch 655

Long and short stitch 702
Running stitch 312
Long and short stitch 302
Satin stitch 346
Satin stitch 2307
French knot stitch 312
Long and short stitch 501
Satin stitch 505A
Satin stitch 263
Satin stitch 346
Satin stitch 346
Backstitch 310

Satin stitch 308
French knot stitch 100 (three strands)
Satin stitch 118
French knot stitch
Satin stitch 310
Satin stitch 444

Backstitch 600

※Unless otherwise specified, use two strands
※Unless otherwise specified use backstitch 312 to work lines (one strand)

Straight stitch 895

Satin stitch 506

BISCUIT

French knot stitch

Satin stitch 600

Running stitch

Satin stitch 308

Long and short stitch 576

Long and short stitch

702

Backstitch 895

214

Work outline stitch in two rows each of 100 and 310 (two strands)

308

310

Satin stitch 816

Satin stitch 346

Long and short stitch 813

Long and short stitch 118

Satin stitch 308

Satin stitch 600

Backstitch 310

Long and short stitch 346

French knot stitch 312 (one strand)

Satin stitch 2311

Satin stitch 631

Long and short stitch 845

Long and short stitch 858

Satin stitch 308

Running stitch 600

French knot stitch 215

Satin stitch 2307

Long and short stitch 2702

Straight stitch 2307

Long and short stitch 311

French knot stitch 312 (one strand)

2563

100

Straight stitch

Satin stitch 600

Long and short stitch

345

Long and short stitch 891

French knot stitch 600

Long and short stitch

118

384

Satin stitch 506

Long and short stitch 574

501

Satin stitch 2105

Long and short stitch 2307

Straight stitch 312

French knot stitch 312 (one strand)

2307

Long and short stitch

Running stitch 312

Long and short stitch 214

Long and short stitch 346

Use backstitch 600 for outline

French knot stitch 346 (one strand)

Lace Patterns

※Use embroidery thread 140
※For couching stitch, use three strands for main stitches and one strand to secure
※For raised blanket stitch, pass thread through fabric three times and make a fine blanket stitch

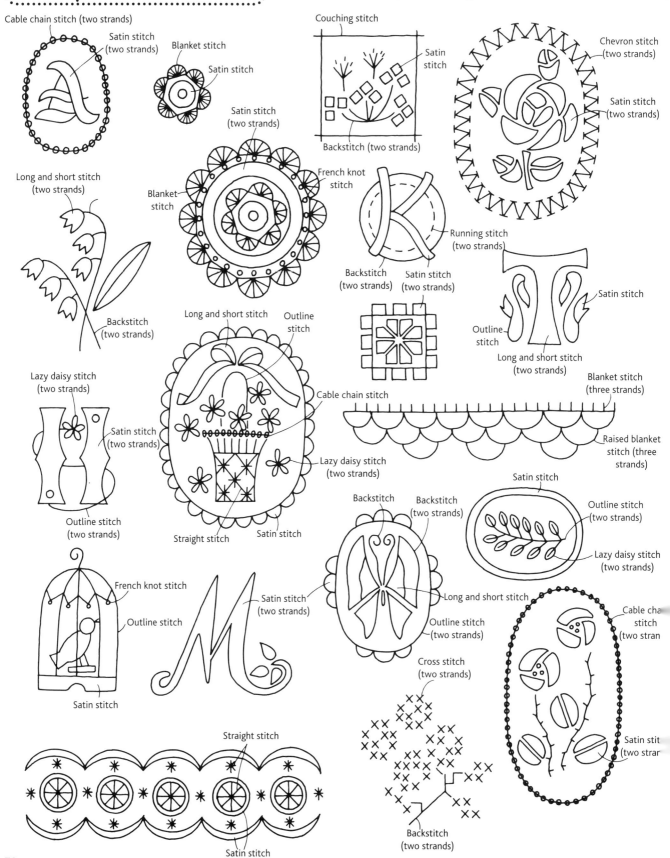

Cable chain stitch (two strands)

Satin stitch (two strands)

Blanket stitch

Satin stitch

Couching stitch

Satin stitch

Backstitch (two strands)

Chevron stitch (two strands)

Satin stitch (two strands)

Satin stitch (two strands)

Blanket stitch

French knot stitch

Long and short stitch (two strands)

Backstitch (two strands)

Running stitch (two strands)

Backstitch (two strands)

Satin stitch (two strands)

Satin stitch

Outline stitch

Long and short stitch (two strands)

Long and short stitch

Outline stitch

Lazy daisy stitch (two strands)

Satin stitch (two strands)

Cable chain stitch

Lazy daisy stitch (two strands)

Blanket stitch (three strands)

Raised blanket stitch (three strands)

Satin stitch

Outline stitch (two strands)

Outline stitch (two strands)

Straight stitch

Satin stitch

Backstitch

Backstitch (two strands)

Lazy daisy stitch (two strands)

French knot stitch

Outline stitch

Satin stitch (two strands)

Long and short stitch

Outline stitch (two strands)

Cable chain stitch (two strands)

Satin stitch

Cross stitch (two strands)

Satin stitch (two strands)

Straight stitch

Satin stitch

Backstitch (two strands)

76

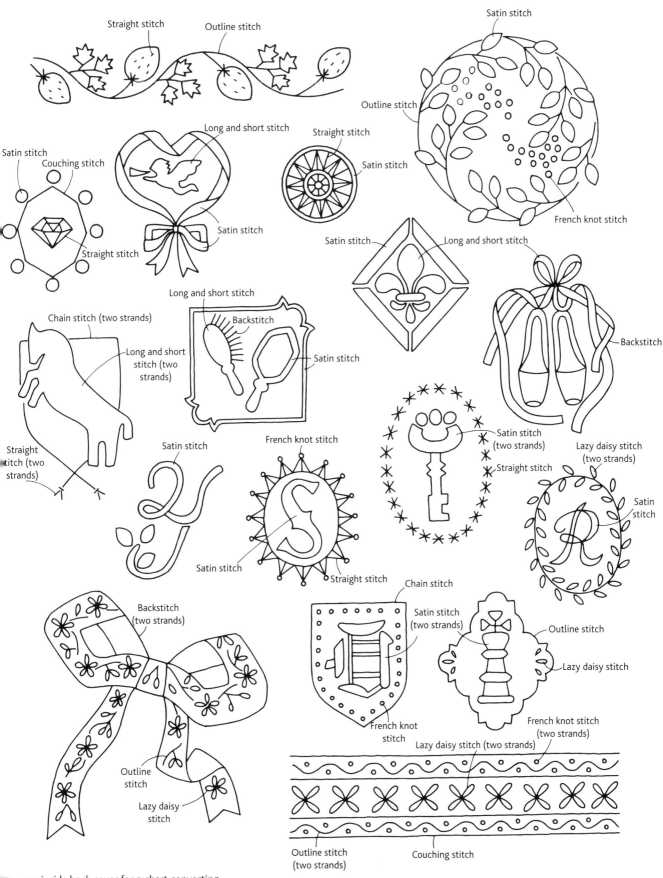

Straight stitch

Outline stitch

Satin stitch

Satin stitch
Couching stitch

Long and short stitch

Straight stitch

Satin stitch

Outline stitch

French knot stitch

Satin stitch

Long and short stitch

Straight stitch

Satin stitch

Chain stitch (two strands)

Long and short stitch

Backstitch

Long and short stitch (two strands)

Satin stitch

Backstitch

Straight stitch (two strands)

Satin stitch

French knot stitch

Satin stitch (two strands)

Straight stitch

Lazy daisy stitch (two strands)

Satin stitch

Satin stitch

Straight stitch

Backstitch (two strands)

Chain stitch

Satin stitch (two strands)

Outline stitch

Lazy daisy stitch

Outline stitch

French knot stitch

French knot stitch (two strands)

Lazy daisy stitch

Lazy daisy stitch (two strands)

Outline stitch (two strands)

Couching stitch

ase see inside back cover for a chart converting
mo brand floss to DMC brand.

The color codes used throughout this book refer to Cosmo brand embroidery floss. Equivalent codes for DMC floss are given in a chart found inside the back cover of this book.

※All designs use two strands

× 107
○ 563

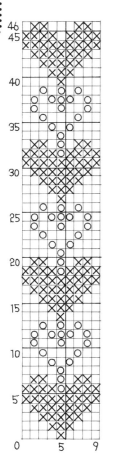

× 242

× 367
○ 310

× 106

× 563   ○ 898

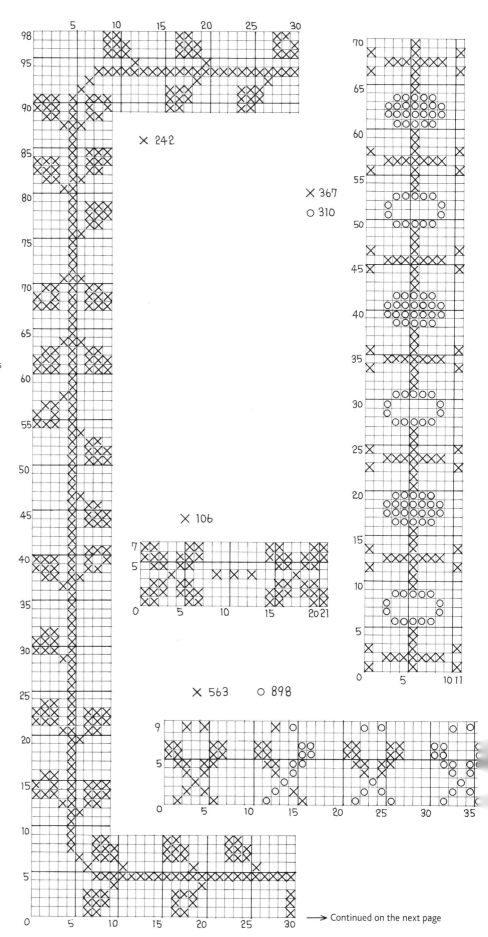

→ Continued on the next page

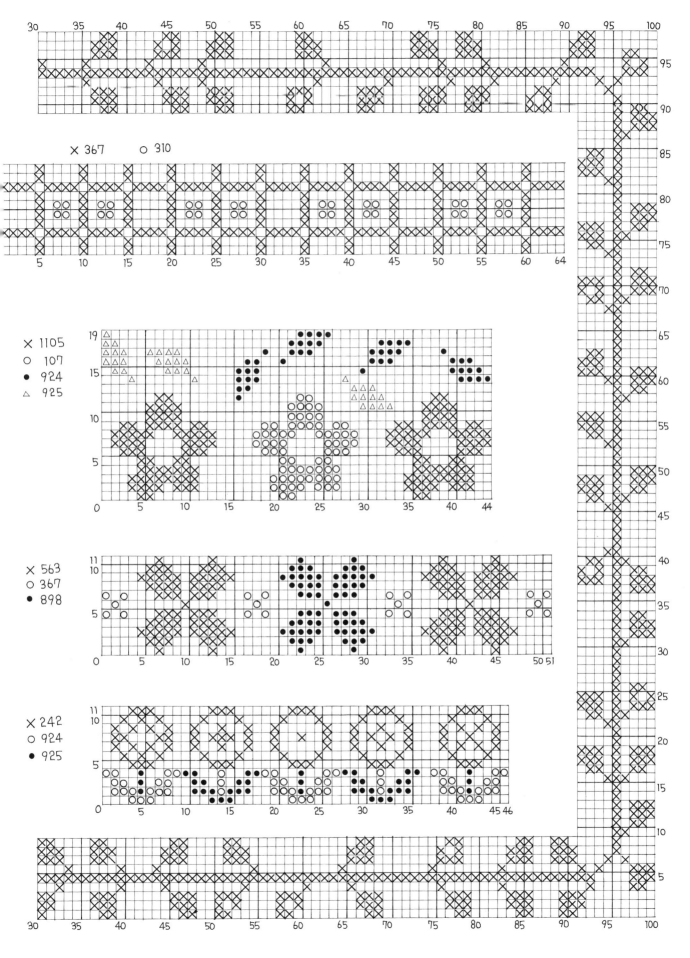

× 367   ○ 310

× 1105
○ 107
● 924
△ 925

× 563
○ 367
● 898

× 242
○ 924
● 925

A Cross Stitch Alphabet

The color codes used throughout this book refer to Cosmo brand embroidery floss. Equivalent codes for DMC floss are given in a chart found inside the back cover of this book.

※All cross stitch 346 (two strands)

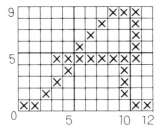
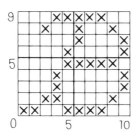
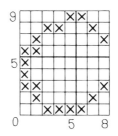
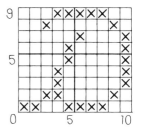

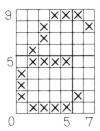
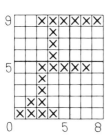
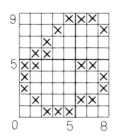
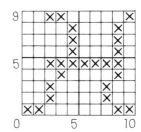
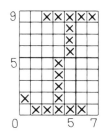

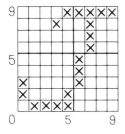
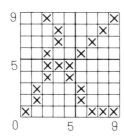
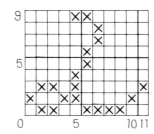
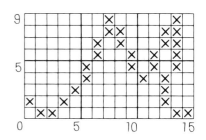

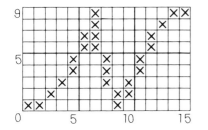
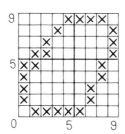
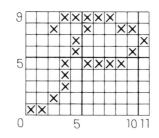
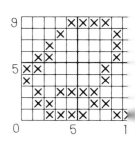

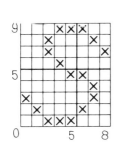

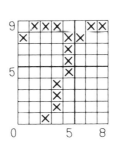

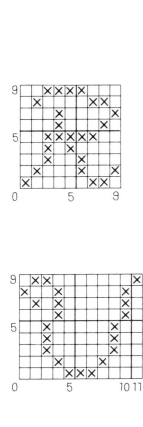

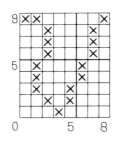

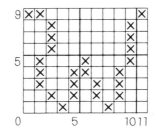

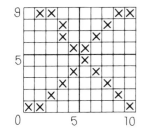

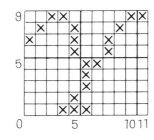

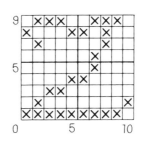

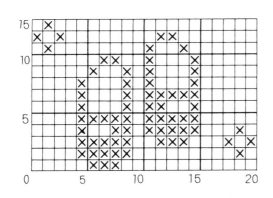

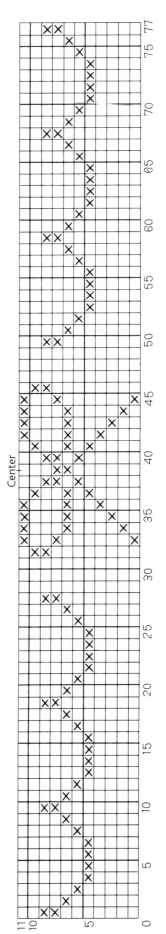

Dog-1

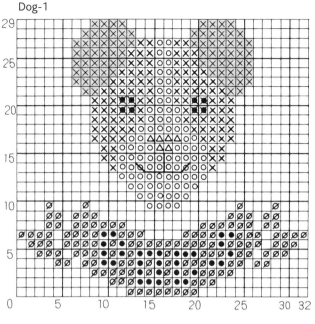

X = 703
o = 1000
⊠ = 705
△ = 2311
✹ = 600
∅ = 215
● = 300

※ Use backstitch for mouth line (three strands)

Dog-2

X = 704 o = 1000 ∅ = 852 ⊠ = 706 △ = 60

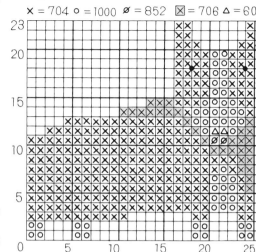

Dog-3

X = 600   o = 715   ※ Use 427 for eyes

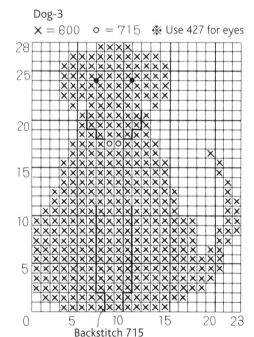

Backstitch 715

Dog-4

X = 427   o = 1000   △ = 600   ⊠ = 23

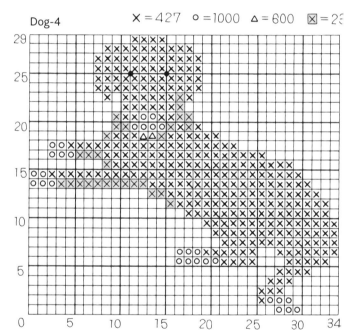

Dog-5

X = 367   o = 1000   △ = 600   ◿ = Straight stitch 600 (n

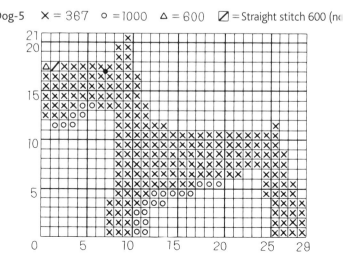

Dog-6

X = 705   o = 345

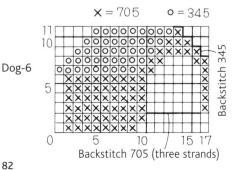

Backstitch 345

Backstitch 705 (three strands)

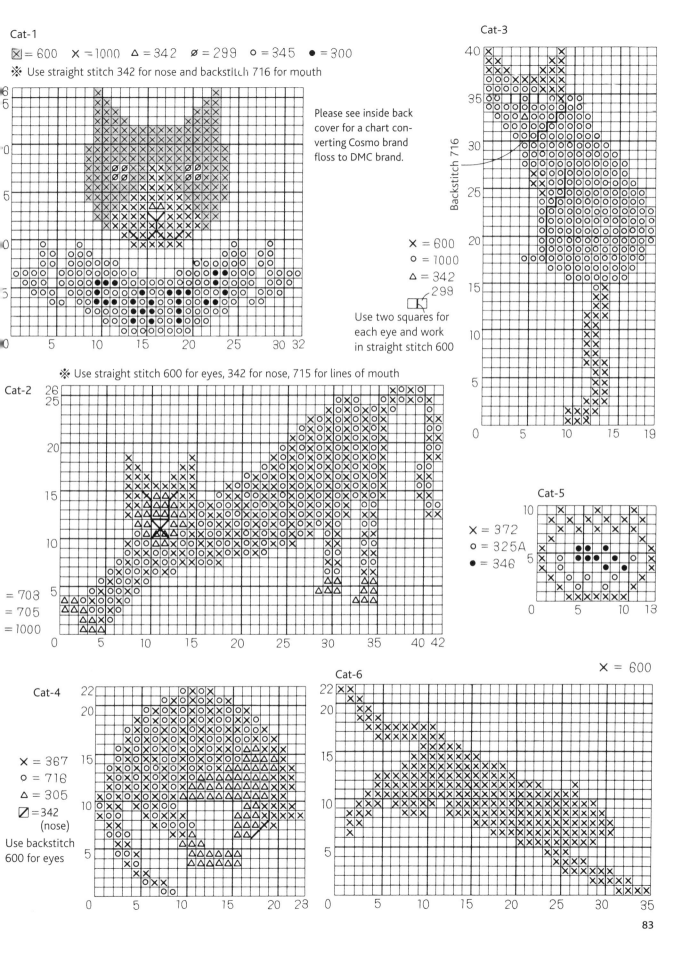

Cat-1

☒ = 600   ✕ =1000   △ = 342   ∅ = 299   ○ = 345   ● = 300

※ Use straight stitch 342 for nose and backstitch 716 for mouth

Please see inside back cover for a chart converting Cosmo brand floss to DMC brand.

✕ = 600
○ = 1000
△ = 342
299

Use two squares for each eye and work in straight stitch 600

Cat-3

Backstitch 716

Cat-2

※ Use straight stitch 600 for eyes, 342 for nose, 715 for lines of mouth

= 703
= 705
= 1000

Cat-5

✕ = 372
○ = 325A
● = 346

✕ = 600

Cat-4

✕ = 367
○ = 716
△ = 305
◨ = 342 (nose)

Use backstitch 600 for eyes

Cat-6

Continuous Cross Stitch Patterns

Please see inside back cover for a chart converting Cosmo brand floss to DMC brand.

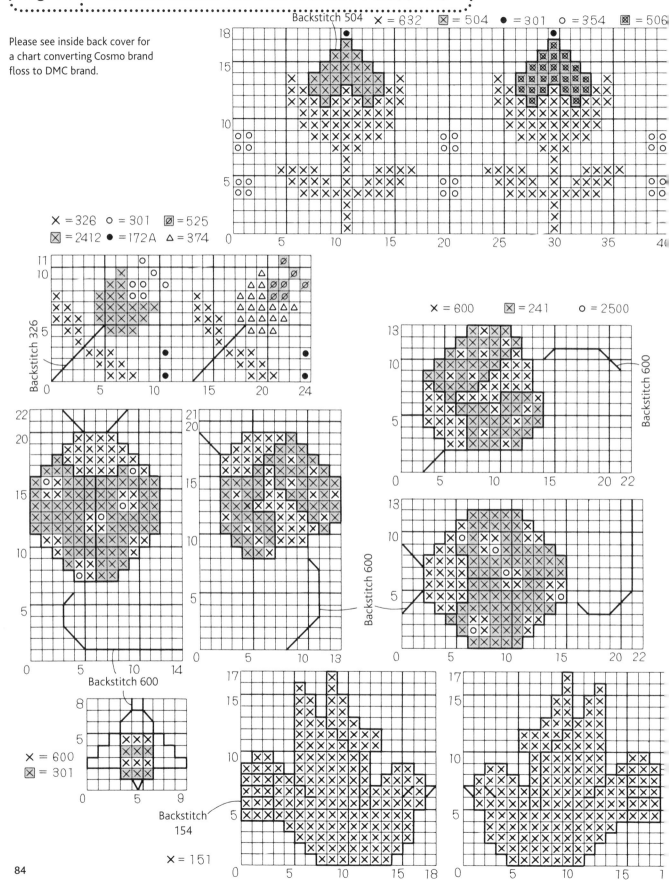

Backstitch 504   ✕ = 632   ☒ = 504   ● = 301   ○ = 354   ☒ = 506

✕ = 326   ○ = 301   ⊘ = 525
☒ = 2412   ● = 172A   △ = 374

Backstitch 326

✕ = 600   ☒ = 241   ○ = 2500

Backstitch 600

Backstitch 600

Backstitch 600

✕ = 600
☒ = 301

Backstitch 154

✕ = 151

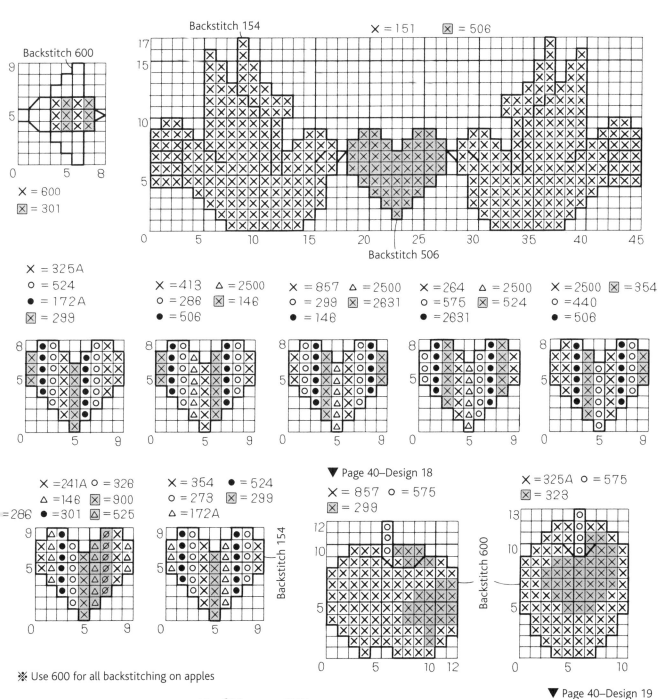

Backstitch 600

Backstitch 154   X = 151   ⊠ = 506

X = 600
⊠ = 301

Backstitch 506

X = 325A
○ = 524
● = 172A
⊠ = 299

X = 413   △ = 2500
○ = 286   ⊠ = 146
● = 506

X = 857   △ = 2500
○ = 299   ⊠ = 2631
● = 146

X = 264   △ = 2500
○ = 575   ⊠ = 524
● = 2631

X = 2500 ⊠ = 354
○ = 440
● = 506

X = 241A ○ = 326
△ = 146   ⊠ = 900
=286 ● = 301 ▱ = 525

X = 354   ● = 524
○ = 273   ⊠ = 299
△ = 172A

▼ Page 40–Design 18
X = 857   ○ = 575
⊠ = 299

Backstitch 154

X = 325A ○ = 575
⊠ = 323

Backstitch 600

※ Use 600 for all backstitching on apples

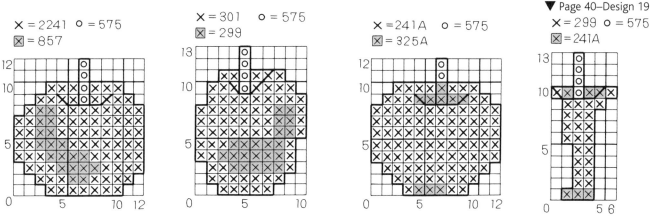

X = 2241 ○ = 575
⊠ = 857

X = 301   ○ = 575
⊠ = 299

X = 241A ○ = 575
⊠ = 325A

▼ Page 40–Design 19
X = 299   ○ = 575
⊠ = 241A

1–3 Stylish Pouches

1·Materials
Fabric (cream linen) 21⅝ in (55cm) wide x 13¾ in (35cm)
No. 25 embroidery thread (264·855)
Ribbon ¼ in (5mm) wide x 25⅝ in (65cm)

2·Materials
Fabric (cream linen) 29½ in (75cm) wide x 19¾ in (50cm)
No. 25 embroidery thread (264·855·1000)
Ribbon ¼ in (5mm) wide x 35½ in (90cm)

3·Materials
Fabric (cream linen) 37½ in (95cm) wide x 25⅝ in (65cm)
No. 25 embroidery thread (264)
Ribbon ¼ in (5mm) wide x 1⅛ yd (1m)

Drafting Pieces

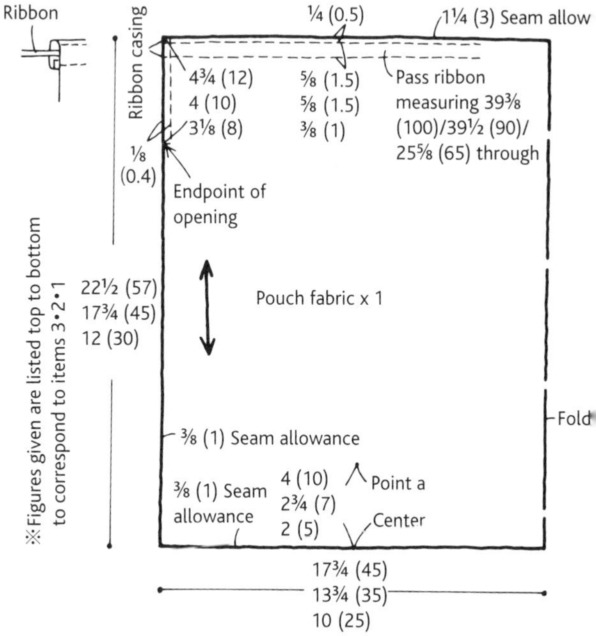

Ribbon

Ribbon casing

※Figures given are listed top to bottom to correspond to items 3·2·1

¼ (0.5)   1¼ (3) Seam allow

4¾ (12)   ⅝ (1.5)   Pass ribbon measuring 39⅜ (100)/39½ (90)/ 25⅝ (65) through
4 (10)   ⅝ (1.5)
3⅛ (8)   ⅜ (1)

⅛ (0.4)

Endpoint of opening

22½ (57)
17¾ (45)
12 (30)

Pouch fabric x 1

Fold

⅜ (1) Seam allowance

⅜ (1) Seam allowance   4 (10)   Point a
                        2¾ (7)
                        2 (5)   Center

17¾ (45)
13¾ (35)
10 (25)

Full-size Diagrams

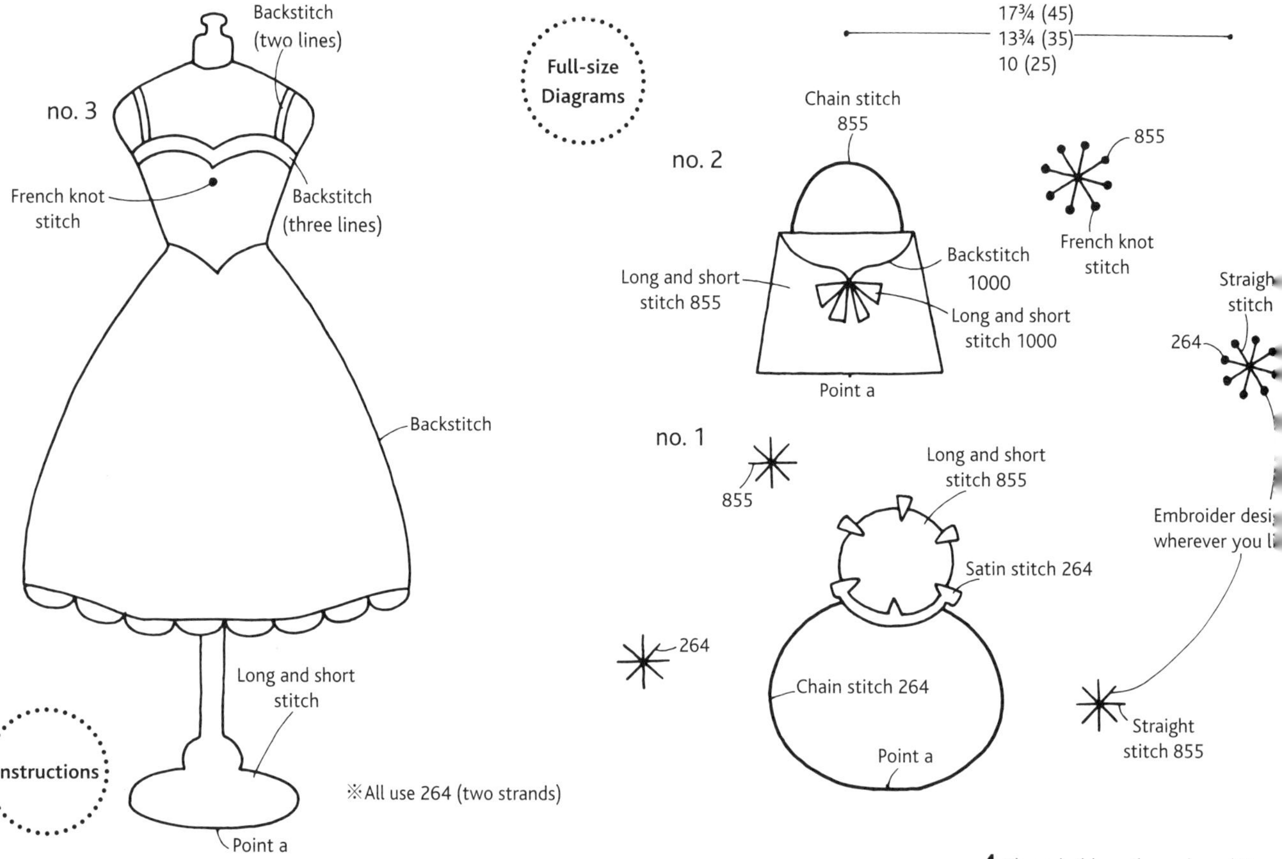

no. 3

Backstitch (two lines)

French knot stitch

Backstitch (three lines)

Backstitch

Long and short stitch

Instructions

Point a

※All use 264 (two strands)

no. 2

Chain stitch 855

Long and short stitch 855

Backstitch 1000

Long and short stitch 1000

Point a

855

French knot stitch

Straight stitch

264

no. 1

Long and short stitch 855

855

Satin stitch 264

264

Chain stitch 264

Point a

Embroider desi wherever you li

Straight stitch 855

1 Embroider design and serge down from below endpoint of opening. Sew around edges.

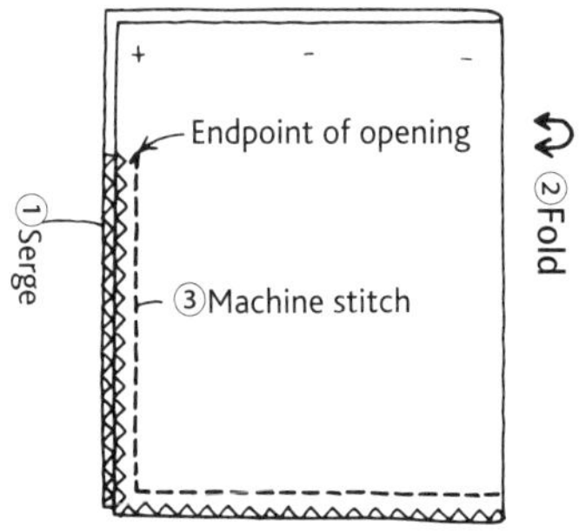

Endpoint of opening

①Serge

③Machine stitch

②Fold

2 Open out seams and sew opening edges.

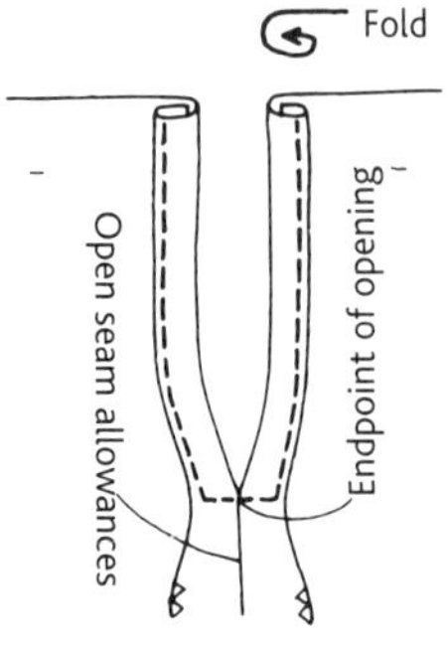

Fold

Open seam allowances

Endpoint of opening

3 Fold casing over and sew.

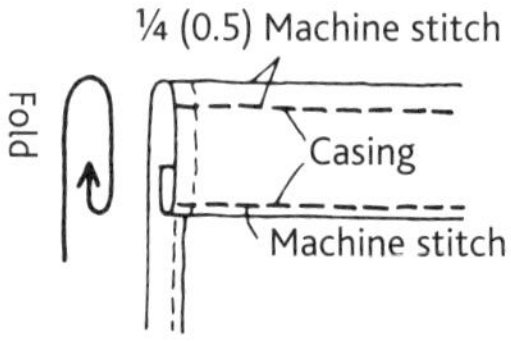

¼ (0.5) Machine stitch

Fold

Casing

Machine stitch

4 Thread ribbon through and tie.

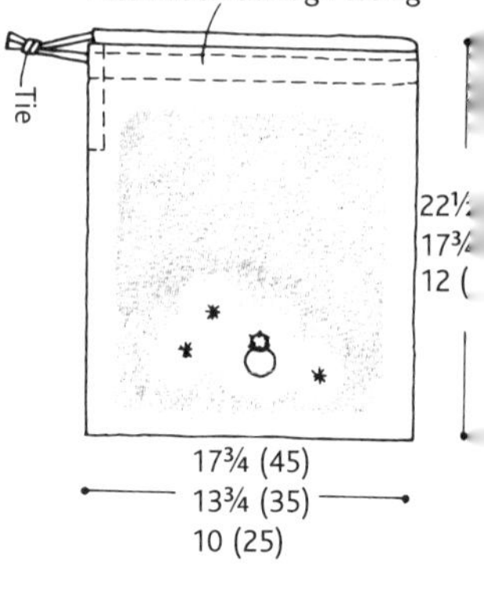

Pass ribbon through casing

Tie

22½
17¾
12 (

17¾ (45)
13¾ (35)
10 (25)

4–7 Self-cover Buttons

Materials (for four buttons)
Fabric (white linen) 4 x 4 in (10×10cm)
No. 25 embroidery thread in
    4 (167•302•800)
    5 (327•574•758)
    6 (311•632•701)
    7 (311•327•800)
Self-cover buttons ⅝ in (1.5cm) in diameter x 4

Instructions

Cut embroidered fabric and cover buttons, using the diagram as a guide for centering design.

Position embroidery in center and cut circle

no. 6   Create self-cover button   no. 7

no. 5   no. 4

---

8 Scissors Case

Materials
Fabric (navy linen) 6 x 4 in (15×10cm)
Tape ⅛ in (3mm) wide x 8 in (20cm)
No. 25 embroidery thread (325A)
Craft wadding
Waste canvas

The color codes used throughout this book refer to Cosmo brand embroidery floss. Equivalent codes for DMC floss are given in a chart found inside the back cover of this book.

Drafting Pieces

Main body piece x 1   Tape x 1

Attach tape here
Embroider on front only
Stuff with wadding
1⅝ (4) Opening for turning
2¾ (7)
Fold
Center
a
5 (2)
8 (20)

Instructions

Diagram

1 Embroider design and cut out fabric.

2 Fold with right sides facing and sew around edges.

3 Turn right side out and stuff with wadding.

③Add seam allowance and cut out
①Embroider design
⅜ (1) Seam allowance
②Place embroidered design in center and decide on stitching line for finished item
a

Sandwich tape between layers
MAIN PIECE (WS)
Fold in half
Leave opening for turning
Sew together

Turn right side out and stuff with wadding
Blind hem stitch opening closed

※Use two strands of 325A

a

87

9 . 10 Pin Cushion

Please see inside back cover for a chart converting Cosmo brand floss to DMC brand.

Instructions

9 · Materials
Fabric (white linen) 3¼ x 5⅛ in (8×13cm)
No. 25 embroidery thread (167)
Small amount of craft wadding
Waste canvas

10 · Materials
Fabric (navy linen) 4 x 7 in (10×18cm)
No. 25 embroidery thread (325A)
Small amount of craft wadding
Waste canvas

Drafting Pieces

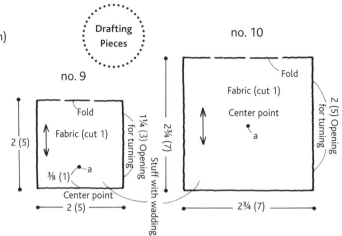

1 Prepare a piece of fabric larger than the design. Embroider the design and trim fabric to pattern size

2 Fold fabric edges together with right side in and sew around edges.

3 Turn right side out and stuff with wadding.

Diagrams

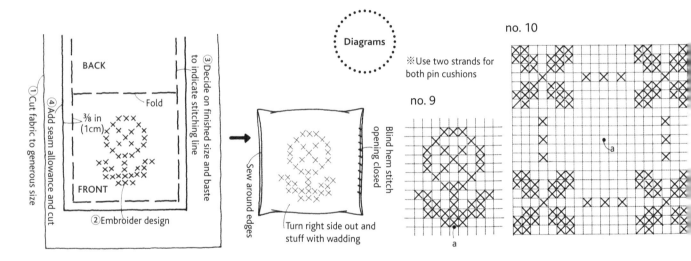

※Use two strands for both pin cushions

---

11 . 12 Camisoles

11 · Materials
Camisole
No. 25 embroidery thread (816)

12 · Materials
Camisole
No. 25 embroidery thread (310・318・836)

● Embroider design where desired on camisole

Full-size Diagrams

※Use two strands for entire design

no. 12

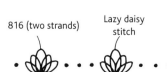
Backstitch 836
French knot stitch 301
Lazy daisy stitch 318
Backstitch 318

no. 11

816 (two strands)
Lazy daisy stitch
French knot stitch

13 · Materials
Fabric (pale blue double gauze) 65 x 21⅝ in (165×55cm)
No. 25 embroidery thread (302·324·415A·798·845)
Lightweight fusible interfacing 4 x 4 in (10×10cm)

14 · Materials
Fabric (white double gauze) 65 x 21⅝ in (165×55cm)
No. 25 embroidery thread (145·214·215·329·423·445·
503·525·600·706·798·800)
Lightweight fusible interfacing 6 x 4 in (15×10cm)

● Cut out fabric pieces roughly, embroider design and
add seam allowances before cutting out to assemble.

Drafting Pieces

Main piece x 1

Fold   Fabric

19¾ (50)

Embroider lower left

⅜ (0.8) Machine stitch

Opening

31½ (80)

Instructions

1 Apply fusible interfacing to fabric and embroider design.

Folding line

Embroider design

Cut seam allowances so pieces match

2 Face right sides together and sew top and bottom. Finish off seam allowances.

Serge through both thicknesses

Machine stitch

Fold

Fold over

FABRIC (WS)

⅝ (2) Seam allowance

⅜ (1) Seam allowance

3 Sew openings.

Fold over twice and machine stitch

Full-size Item

no. 13

3½ (9)

4 (10)

Pillow case

no. 14

4 (10)

4 (10)

mléčná

※Unless otherwise specified, use two strands
※Use straight stitch 600 for nose and eyebrows
※Use satin stitch 600 for eyes

Full-size Diagrams

no. 13

Blanket stitch 798

Straight stitch 302

Satin stitch 798

Straight stitch 845

Satin stitch 302

Satin stitch 302

Satin stitch 415A

Satin stitch 845

Satin stitch 324

Backstitch 845

Satin stitch 845

Satin stitch 324

no.14

Satin stitch 798

445   503

145   525

145

525

445

503

Backstitch 423

Satin stitch 329

Satin stitch 706

French knot stitch 214

Backstitch 214

Satin stitch 215

329

Backstitch 800

mléčná

※Use backstitch 329 for stems (one strand)

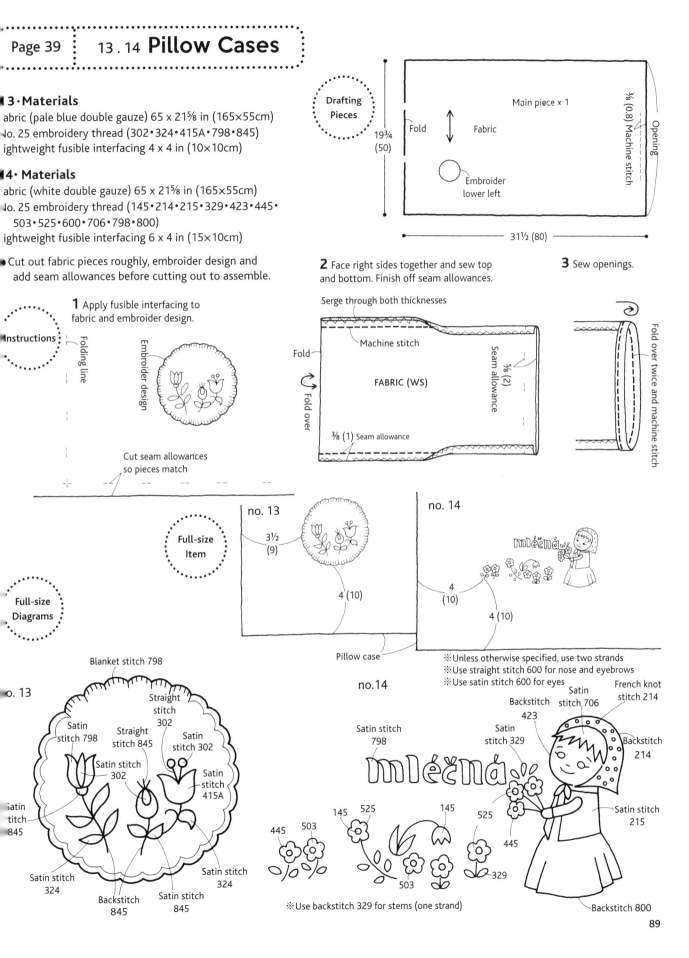

Materials
No. 25 embroidery thread (800)

● Embroider design where desired on blouse.
● For articles that will be washed frequently,
  it's fine to start and finish stitching with a knot.

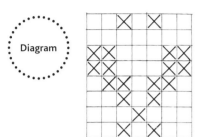

Diagram

※Cross stitch 800
(two strands)

16・Materials
No. 25 embroidery thread (312)

17・Materials
No. 25 embroidery thread (167・2307)

● Embroider design wherever you like on the handkerchief.
● For articles that will be washed frequently, it's fine to start and finish stitching with a knot.

Full-size Diagrams

no. 16

Outline stitch
312 (one strand)

no. 17

Outline stitch
2307 (one strand)

French knot stitch
167 (one strand)

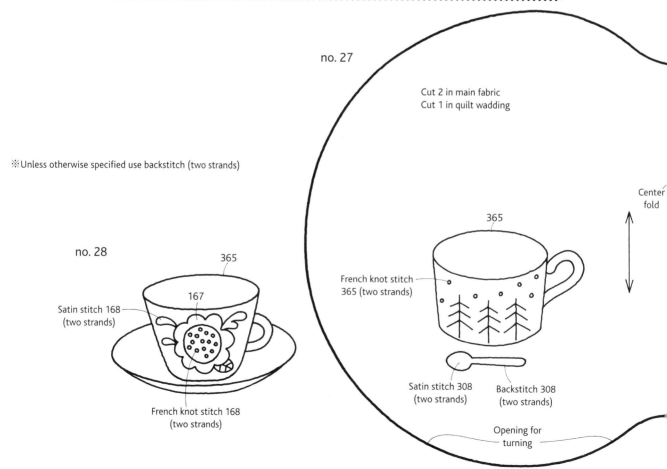

no. 27

Cut 2 in main fabric
Cut 1 in quilt wadding

※Unless otherwise specified use backstitch (two strands)

Center fold

365

French knot stitch
365 (two strands)

Satin stitch 308
(two strands)

Backstitch 308
(two strands)

Opening for turning

no. 28

365

167

Satin stitch 168
(two strands)

French knot stitch 168
(two strands)

90

Page 41 **20 . 21 Dishcloth**

Materials

No. 25 embroidery thread in 20 (312・345・704)
21 (312・345・704)

● Embroider design wherever you like on the cloth
● For articles that will be washed frequently,
   it's fine to start and finish stitching with a knot.

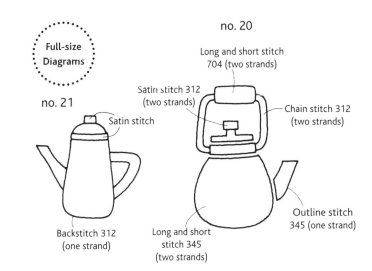

Full-size Diagrams

no. 21

no. 20

Satin stitch

Long and short stitch 704 (two strands)

Satin stitch 312 (two strands)

Chain stitch 312 (two strands)

Backstitch 312 (one strand)

Long and short stitch 345 (two strands)

Outline stitch 345 (one strand)

Page 41 **22 Café Apron**

Materials

One dishcloth
Tape 1 in (2.5cm) wide x 2¼ yd (2m)
No. 25 embroidery thread (166・311・345・703)

Attach tape to dishcloth and embroider cloth
For articles that will be washed frequently, it's fine to
   start and finish stitching with a knot.

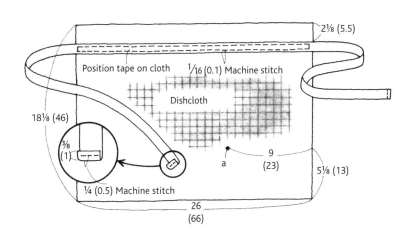

2⅛ (5.5)

Position tape on cloth

¹/₁₆ (0.1) Machine stitch

Dishcloth

18⅛ (46)

⅜ (1)

¼ (0.5) Machine stitch

9 (23)

a

5⅛ (13)

26 (66)

The color codes used throughout this book
refer to Cosmo brand embroidery floss.
Equivalent codes for DMC floss are given in a
chart found inside the back cover of this book.

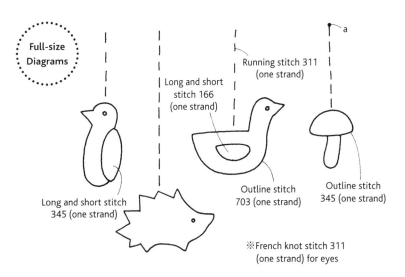

Full-size Diagrams

a

Running stitch 311 (one strand)

Long and short stitch 166 (one strand)

Long and short stitch 345 (one strand)

Outline stitch 703 (one strand)

Outline stitch 345 (one strand)

※French knot stitch 311 (one strand) for eyes

Please see inside back cover for a chart converting Cosmo brand floss to DMC brand.

18·Materials

Fabric (light green linen) 23⅝ in (60cm) wide x 23⅝ in (60cm)
Contrast fabric (checked linen) 10 in (25cm) wide x 10 in (25cm)
Lining (gingham) 31½ in (80cm) wide x 10 in (25cm)

Fusible quilt wadding 31½ in (80cm) wide x 19¾ (50cm)
Lace ½ in (1.3cm) wide x 33½ (85cm)
No. 25 embroidery thread (575·857·299)
Waste canvas

19·Materials

Fabric (light green linen) 8 in (20cm) wide x 8 in (20cm)
Contrast fabric (checked linen) 8 in (20cm) wide x 8 in (20cm)
Fusible quilt wadding 8 in (20cm) wide x 8 in (20cm)
No. 25 embroidery thread (241A·299·575)
Waste canvas

Drafting Pieces

no. 18
Main piece (cut 3)
Cut 2 in main fabric; cut 1 in contrast fabric; cut 6 in fusible quilt wadding; cut 3 in lining

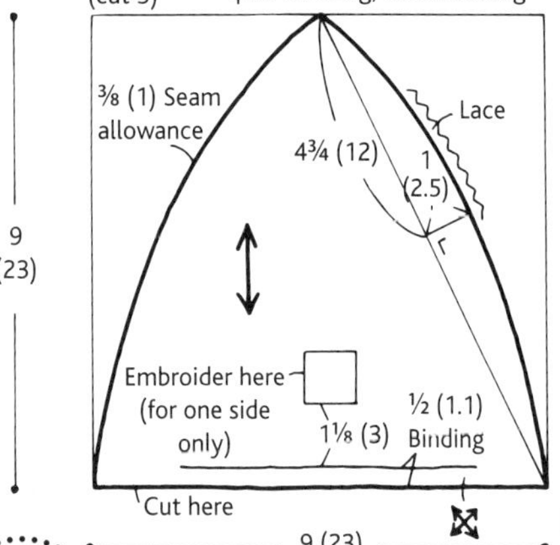

⅜ (1) Seam allowance
Lace
4¾ (12)
1 (2.5)
9 (23)
Embroider here (for one side only)
1⅛ (3)
½ (1.1) Binding
Cut here
9 (23)

Tab (cut 1 from main fabric)
Cut here
3½ (9)
2⅜ (6)

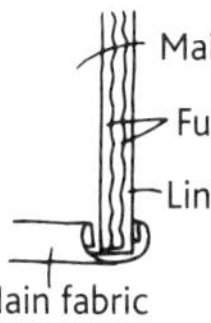

Main fabric
Fusible quilt wadding
Lining fabric
Main fabric

Full-size design on p85 (for both)

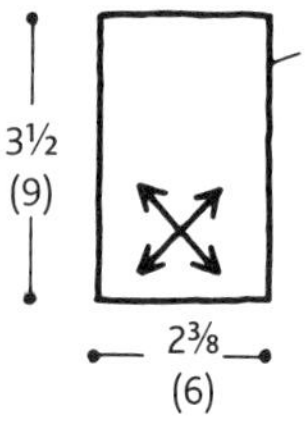

no.19
Main piece (cut 1 each in main fabric, contrast fabric and fusible quilt wadding)

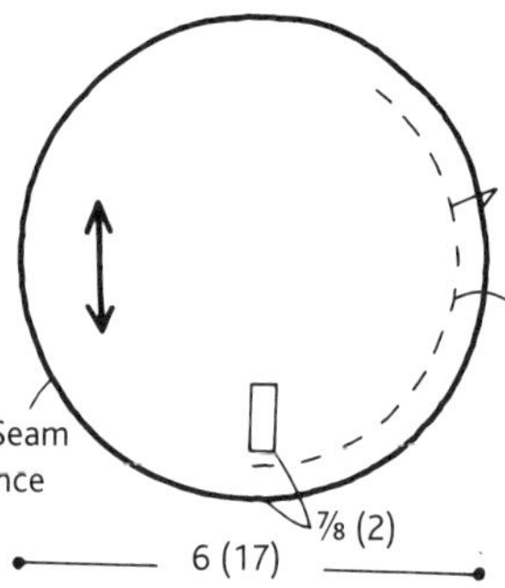

Main fabric
Contrast fabric
Quilt wadding
⅜ (1)
Running stitch
⅜ (1) Seam allowance
⅞ (2)
6 (17)

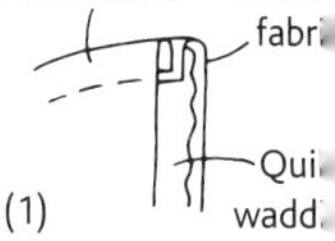

Instructions No. 18

1 Embroider design on main fabric and apply quilt wadding. Attach lace to seam allowance with ⅜ in (1cm) extending.

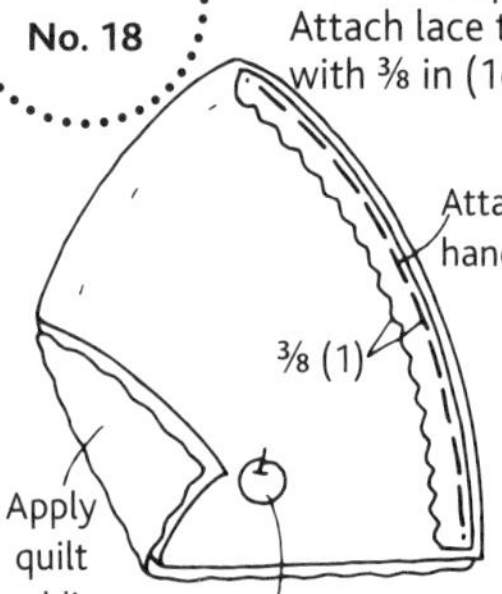

Attach lace to right hand side only
⅜ (1)
Apply quilt wadding
Embroider design, using waste canvas

2 Match two main pieces and sew together.

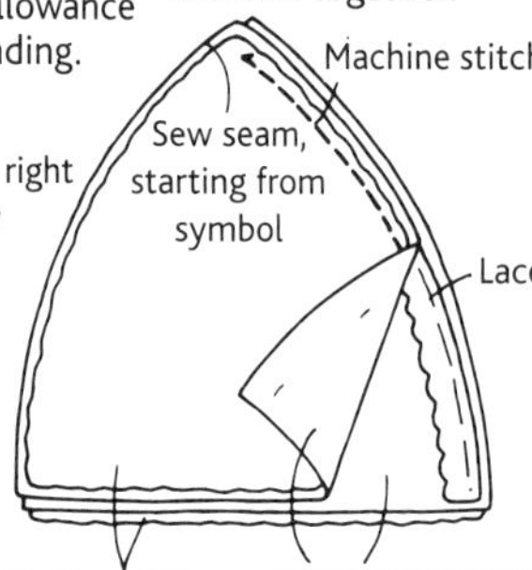

Machine stitch
Sew seam, starting from symbol
Lace
Quilt wadding
MAIN FABRIC (RS)

3 Sew remaining main piece to first two main pieces.

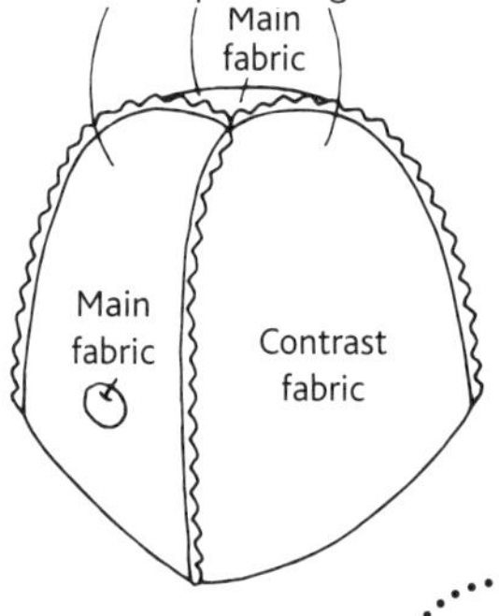

Sew three pieces together
Main fabric
Main fabric
Contrast fabric

4 Apply quilt wadding to lining and sew all three pieces together.

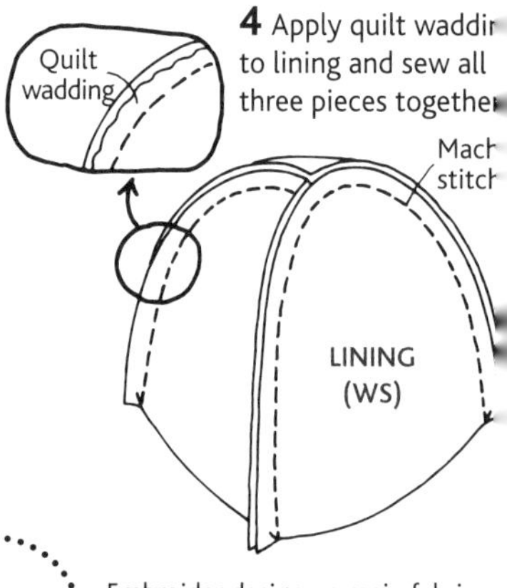

Quilt wadding
Machine stitch
LINING (WS)

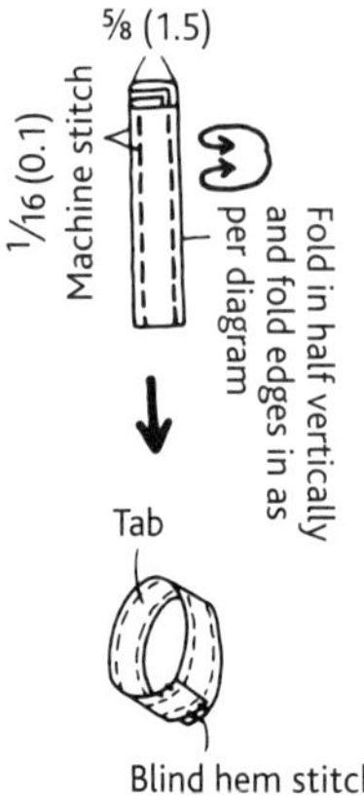

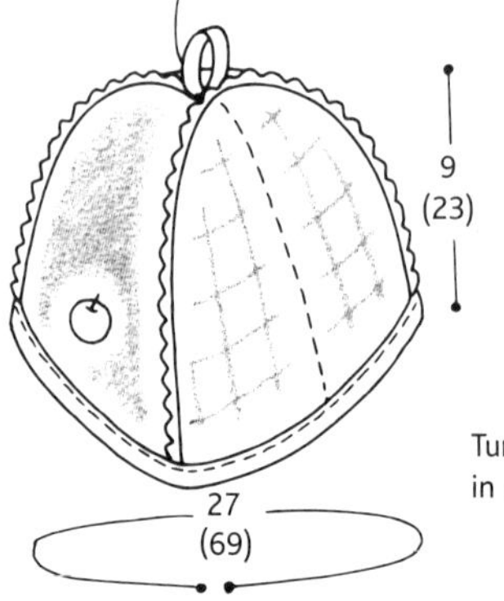

Instructions No. 19

Embroider design on main fabric. Layer quilt wadding and contrast fabric and sew around edges.

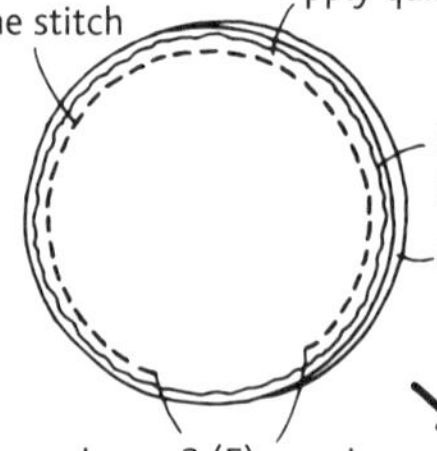

Machine stitch
Apply quilt wadding
EMBROIDERED MAIN FABRIC (WS)
CONTRAST FABRIC (RS)
Leave 2 (5) opening for turning
Sew running stitch 241A through all layers to contrast fabric

5 Insert lining into main piece and bind opening edges.

Sew running stitch 857 through all layers to lining
Contrast fabric
(RS)
Insert lining
Baste

Machine stitch
Binding

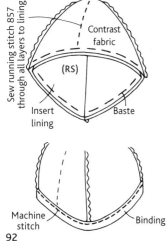

6 Create tab and blind hem stitch to main piece.

⅝ (1.5)
1/16 (0.1) Machine stitch
Fold in half vertically and fold edges in as per diagram
Tab

Blind hem stitch

Attach tab to main section using blind hem stitch
9 (23)
27 (69)

Turn right side out and stitch in running stitch all around

Turn right side out and blind hem stitch opening closed

92

23·Materials

Fabric (linen) 12 in (30cm) wide x 8 in (20cm)
Contrast fabric (cotton in a purple shade with floral
    pattern) 6 in (15cm) wide x 8 in (20cm)
Quilt wadding 12 in (30cm) wide x 8 in (20cm)
No. 25 embroidery thread (556)

24·Materials

Fabric (gauze with pink polka dots) 12 in (30cm)
    wide x 8 in (20cm)
Contrast fabric (cotton with floral pattern) 6 in (15cm)
    wide x 8 in (20cm)
Quilt wadding 12 in (30cm) wide x 8 in (20cm)
No. 25 embroidery thread (312)

Instructions

1 Embroider design.

2 Match main fabric and contrast fabric and sew together.

Turn right side out and blind hem stitch opening closed. Sew running stitch along seams.

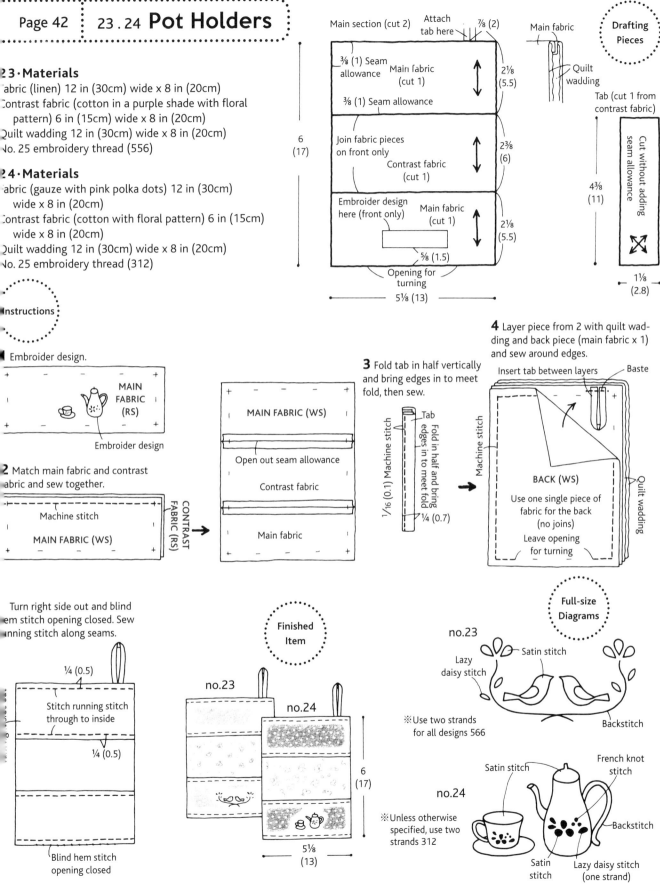

Drafting Pieces

Main section (cut 2)
Attach tab here
⅞ (2)
Main fabric
Quilt wadding

⅜ (1) Seam allowance
Main fabric (cut 1)
⅜ (1) Seam allowance
2⅛ (5.5)

Join fabric pieces on front only
Contrast fabric (cut 1)
2⅜ (6)

Embroider design here (front only)
Main fabric (cut 1)
2⅛ (5.5)

⅝ (1.5)
Opening for turning
5⅛ (13)
6 (17)

Tab (cut 1 from contrast fabric)
Cut without adding seam allowance
4⅜ (11)
1⅛ (2.8)

3 Fold tab in half vertically and bring edges in to meet fold, then sew.

Tab
Fold in half and bring edges in to meet fold
1/16 (0.1) Machine stitch
¼ (0.7)

4 Layer piece from 2 with quilt wadding and back piece (main fabric x 1) and sew around edges.

Insert tab between layers
Baste
Machine stitch
BACK (WS)
Use one single piece of fabric for the back (no joins)
Leave opening for turning
Quilt wadding

MAIN FABRIC (RS)
Embroider design

Machine stitch
MAIN FABRIC (WS)
CONTRAST FABRIC (RS)

MAIN FABRIC (WS)
Open out seam allowance
Contrast fabric
Main fabric

¼ (0.5)
Stitch running stitch through to inside
¼ (0.5)
Blind hem stitch opening closed

Finished Item
no.23
no.24
6 (17)
5⅛ (13)

Full-size Diagrams

no.23
Satin stitch
Lazy daisy stitch
Backstitch
※Use two strands for all designs 566

no.24
Satin stitch
French knot stitch
Backstitch
Satin stitch
Lazy daisy stitch (one strand)
※Unless otherwise specified, use two strands 312

2 5 · Materials

Fabric (purple checked linen)
19¾ (50cm) wide x 19¾ (50cm)
No. 25 embroidery thread (266•895•2224)

2 6 · Materials

Fabric (purple cotton gingham) 15¾ (40cm) wide x 15¾ (40cm)
No. 25 embroidery thread (118•375•857)

Full-size Diagram

no. 25

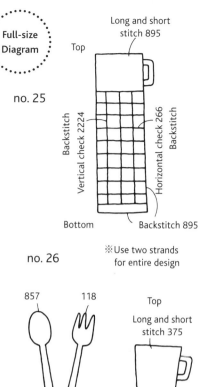

Drafting Pieces

Instructions

Machine stitch around edges and embroider design.

Fold over twice

1/16 (0.1)

(WS)

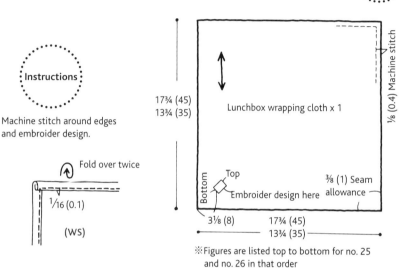

17¾ (45)
13¾ (35)

Lunchbox wrapping cloth x 1

⅛ (0.4) Machine stitch
Drafting stitch

Bottom

Top

Embroider design here

⅜ (1) Seam allowance

3⅛ (8)   17¾ (45)
13¾ (35)

※Figures are listed top to bottom for no. 25 and no. 26 in that order

no. 26

※Use two strands for entire design

857   118

Backstitch

Top
Long and short stitch 375

Bottom

Backstitch

※Use two strands for entire design

Materials

Fabric (peppermint green cotton with polka dots) 25⅝ in (65cm) wide x 21⅝ in (55cm)
No. 25 embroidery thread (373, 383)

Drafting Pieces

Instructions

Machine stitch around edges and embroider design.

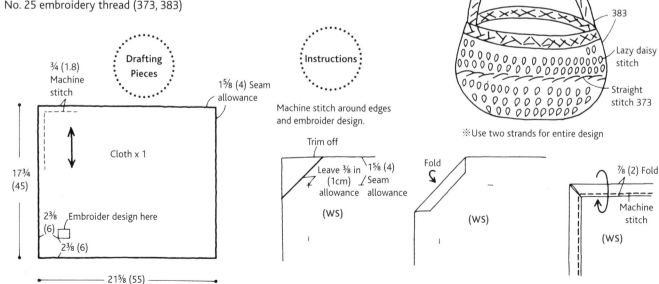

¾ (1.8) Machine stitch

1⅝ (4) Seam allowance

Cloth x 1

17¾ (45)

2⅜ (6)   Embroider design here

2⅜ (6)

21⅝ (55)

Trim off

Leave ⅜ in (1cm) Seam allowance

1⅝ (4) Seam allowance

(WS)

Fold

(WS)

⅞ (2) Fold

Machine stitch

(WS)

Backstitch

383

Lazy daisy stitch

Straight stitch 373

※Use two strands for entire design

94

Materials (same requirements for each pot holder)

Fabric(plain) 19⅝ x 6 in (50×15cm)
Quilt wadding 10 x 6 in (25×15cm)
¼ in (5mm) wide ribbon x 21⅝ in (55cm)
No. 25 embroidery thread in 27 (308・365)
28 (167・168・365)

See p90 for full-size designs and pattern

For articles that will be washed frequently, it's fine to start and finish stitching with a knot

Instructions

1 Embroider design. Cut seam allowances so pieces match.

2 Layer wadding and fabric as per diagram and sew around edges.

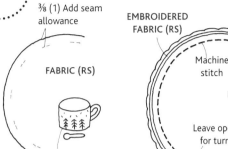

⅜ (1) Add seam allowance

FABRIC (RS)

Embroider onto roughly cut out fabric pieces

EMBROIDERED FABRIC (RS)

Wadding

Machine stitch

⅜ (1) Seam allowance

FABRIC (WS)

Leave opening for turning

Clip into seam allowance

3 Trim seam allowances so pieces match.

②Trim seam allowances to ¼ (0.5)

(WS)

①Trim off wadding in seam allowance

4 Turn right side out and attach ribbon.

Turn right side out

Ribbon 21⅝ in (55cm) long

FABRIC (RS)

③Machine stitch

①Blind hem stitch opening for turning

②Fold ribbon in half and pass over each side of pot holder

Finished Item

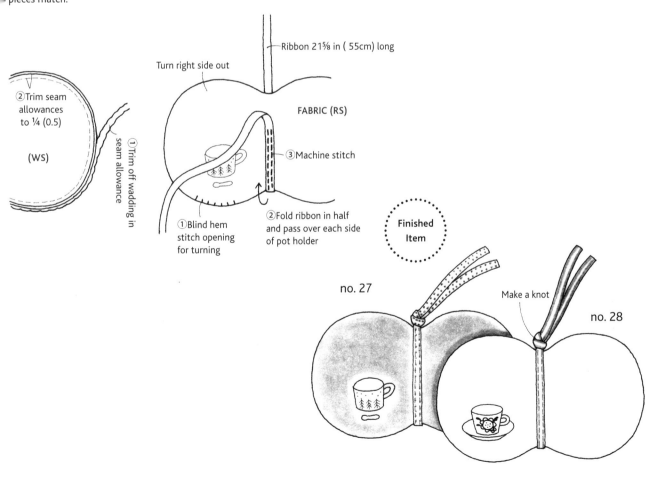

no. 27

Make a knot

no. 28

95

Published in 2016 by Tuttle Publishing, an imprint of
Periplus Editions (HK) Ltd.

www.tuttlepublishing.com

Library of Congress Control Number: 2015951250
ISBN 978-4-8053-1376-3

Chiisana Shishuu Zuan to Komono
Copyright © Boutique-Sha, Inc. 2011
English Translation rights arranged with BOUTIQUE-SHA, INC.
through Japan, UNI Agency, Inc., Tokyo

English Translation © 2016 Periplus Editions (HK) Ltd.
Translated from Japanese by Leeyong Soo
All rights reserved.

Original Japanese edition:
Design: s@chi, Sareee, Campanella, Satomi Fujita
Photography: Miwa Kumon
Step-by-step photography: Ayumi Nakatsuji
Book design: Mihoko Amano, Nanako Futoda
Editors: Kyoko Nishida, Tomoko Kodera (Gakken Publishing);
    Shuko Sato (Little Bird)

Distributed by

North America, Latin America & Europe
Tuttle Publishing
364 Innovation Drive, North Clarendon, VT 05759-9436 U.S.A.
Tel: 1 (802) 773-8930; Fax: 1 (802) 773-6993
info@tuttlepublishing.com
www.tuttlepublishing.com

Japan
Tuttle Publishing
Yaekari Building, 3rd Floor, 5-4-12 Osaki, Shinagawa-ku, Tokyo 141 00
Tel: (81) 3 5437-0171; Fax: (81) 3 5437-0755
sales@tuttle.co.jp
www.tuttle.co.jp

Asia Pacific
Berkeley Books Pte. Ltd.
61 Tai Seng Avenue #02-12, Singapore 534167
Tel: (65) 6280-1330; Fax: (65) 6280-6290
inquiries@periplus.com.sg
www.periplus.com

Printed in Malaysia   1510TW
18 17 16 15   10 9 8 7 6 5 4 3 2 1

TUTTLE PUBLISHING® is a registered trademark of Tuttle Publishing,
a division of Periplus Editions (HK) Ltd.

About Tuttle "Books to Span the East and West"

Our core mission at Tuttle Publishing is to create books which bring people together one page at a time. Tuttle was founded in 1832 in the small New England town of Rutland, Vermont (USA). Our fundamental values remain as strong today as they were then—to publish best-in-class books informing the English-speaking world about the countries and peoples of Asia. The world has become a smaller place today and Asia's economic, cultural and political influence has expanded, yet the need for meaningful dialogue and information about this diverse region has never been greater. Since 1948, Tuttle has been a leader in publishing books on the cultures, arts, cuisines, languages and literatures of Asia. Our authors and photographers have won numerous awards and Tuttle has published thousands of books on subjects ranging from martial arts to paper crafts. We welcome you to explore the wealth of information available on Asia at **www.tuttlepublishing.com**